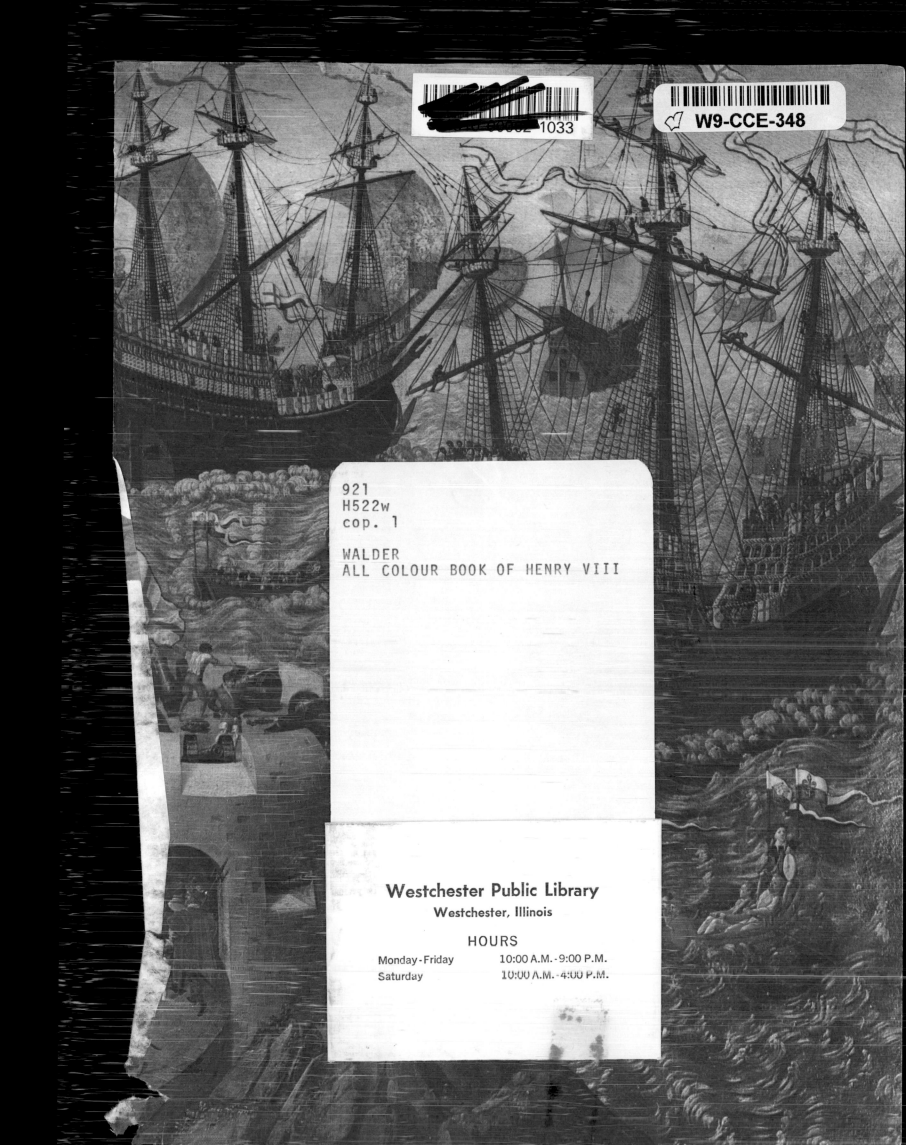

all colour book of

Henry VIII

John Walder

Octopus Books

First published 1973 by
Octopus Books Limited
59 Grosvenor Street, London W1
ISBN 0 7064 0232 4
© 1973 Octopus Books Limited

Distributed in USA by
Crescent Books
a division of Crown Publishers Inc
419 Park Avenue South
New York, N.Y. 10016

Distributed in Australia by
Rigby Limited
30 North Terrace, Kent Town
Adelaide, South Australia 5067

Produced by Mandarin Publishers Limited
14 Westlands Road, Quarry Bay, Hong Kong
Printed in Hong Kong

The Meeting between Henry VIII and Maximilian I (1513) *(see pages 16-17)*

Contents

The Young Henry

In 1509 Henry VII had been on the throne for twenty-four years. By sheer political ability he had turned his reign into an unqualified success. From the dubious victory of Bosworth which confirmed him as just one more in a depressing line of successful usurpers, he had become the founder of a dynasty that within his own lifetime was respected, if not with affection, certainly through a realization of self-interest both at home and abroad.

Quite apart from the immediate task of putting down armed challenges to his throne which came from within the realm, Henry had to overcome the long-term problem of gaining acceptance for his line and of establishing its respectability in the eyes of the world. His approach to this was two-fold: first, he sought the elimination of rival claimants to the throne, and secondly, he pursued a policy of alliance by marriage with the established monarchies of Europe. By 1499, with the execution of the Earl of Warwick, he had largely settled the validity of his own claim to the throne; while this event simultaneously removed the final obstacle to his project for securing the succession.

Henry had married Elizabeth of York at the beginning of his reign to counter-balance the poverty of his own hereditary claim to the throne and to appease the Yorkist interest. Throughout the 1490's he had been engaged in protracted negotiations with Ferdinand and Isabella of Spain for the betrothal of the eldest son of this marriage, Arthur, Prince of Wales, to their daughter Catherine of Aragon. While they were in principle in favour of this match, Ferdinand and Isabella had procrastinated because of their doubts concerning the stability of the Tudor monarchy. In 1499 however, the Spanish ambassador had been able to report, somewhat prematurely, that 'not a doubtful drop of Royal blood remains in this kingdom.' The negotiations were concluded forthwith and the Princess arrived in England. A few years later, when it was a question of remarrying Catherine to her brother-in-law, Henry, there were no such doubts on the part of the Spanish. Indeed, Ferdinand and Isabella were at pains to enlist the Pope's aid in order that this marriage should take place. The success of the Spanish alliance was followed during the early years of the century by the marriage of Henry's

Right
The Family of Henry VII and St George
This picture, painted probably in 1509 to mark the achievements of Henry VII, shows him at prayer with his wife and children. On the left, behind Henry, are his three sons Arthur, Henry and Edmund, his Queen Elizabeth of York and their daughters Margaret, Elizabeth, Mary and Catherine are on the right. Of course, by 1509 only Henry, his second son, and daughters Margaret and Mary were still alive. The figure of St George in the background represents what is a continuous national theme running through the reigns of both Henry VII and Henry VIII, epitomized in the building of St George's Chapel at Windsor.

elder daughter, Margaret, to James IV of Scotland, and by the betrothal of his younger daughter Mary, to Charles, the grandson of the Emperor Maximilian. In dynastic terms the Tudors had arrived.

Henry VII was well aware that the survival of his monarchy did not only depend upon these considerations: it had also to maintain a degree of financial independence. It is a measure of Henry's ability in this sphere that he transformed a bankrupt monarchy into one of the richest in Europe, and on his death left an enormous fortune in the royal coffers. To achieve this feat meant that Henry had had to tread a careful path through the tangle of European diplomacy, and had thereby managed to avoid the financial drain of war. At home he had exercised a stringent control over financial affairs, and had employed men who were above all good at extracting money from unwilling subjects.

Yet despite their reluctance to pay taxes and other dues, many Englishmen had rallied to the throne. For a variety of reasons they were heartily glad to see an end to the years of turmoil. If he was not completely the dull and drab figure that Francis Bacon described, it was certainly not a magnetic personality or a flamboyant royalty that attracted them to Henry. Above all he represented stability and peace, and for twenty-four years he struggled with continuing success to provide just that. By the end of Henry's reign however, many men had forgotten or had never known the chaos of the Wars of the Roses, and were looking for a change. For those who found themselves at the centre of national life, stability was no longer enough to justify the enormous price they had to pay in taxes to swell the Royal budget. Many looked back to the days of Edward IV and his court and compared it favourably with that of Henry VII, which, particularly since the death of Elizabeth of York, had become drab and gloomy, and where there had been no spectacle of note since the marriage of Prince Arthur in 1501. Certainly Henry, aged beyond his fifty-three years by the incessant struggle of his reign, showed no sign of wishing to emulate the splendour of many of the European courts which were establishing a reputation as centres of intellectual and cultural life. On his death, hopes for such change centred upon the figure of his son, the young Prince Henry, and with all apparent reason.

The eighteen-year-old youth who ascended the throne in April 1509, was endowed with all the qualities one could have hoped for in a Renaissance Prince. Tall and well-proportioned, with a very well-shaped leg (admirably set off by the fashions of those days) and very handsome, he dominated the people who made up his court. Yet if he towered above them he was not aloof from them as his father had been. On the contrary Henry VIII had considerable charm and was eager to please. And please he did; for in his character there was something for all to admire. He was a keen horseman and a passionate huntsman; he jousted with skill and enthusiasm. At the same time he was a gifted musician, a singer and a poet producing verse and music which is sung and played to this day. In intellectual matters he could debate theology and discuss the arts with their most learned exponents. A few years later he was to earn from the Pope the title of Defender of the Faith for his defence of the Papacy in his book *Assertio Septem Sacramentorum* against the attacks of Luther. In social life he was the instigator and the leader of the continual festivities which occupied the early years of his court. He displayed great gallantry towards the ladies, and yet maintained an ease of manner with those of inferior rank that made him enormously popular with the public at large.

News of this hitherto little-known paradigm of princely virtues was quickly spread abroad, not least by that small band of Renaissance men which had grouped itself around the King's grandmother, Margaret Beaufort. One of these, Lord Mountjoy, wrote to his friend Erasmus: 'O my Erasmus, if you could see how all the world here is rejoicing in the possession of so great a Prince, how his life is all their desire, you could not contain your tears for joy. The heavens laugh, the earth exults, all things are full of milk, of honey and of nectar! Avarice is expelled from the country; liberality scatters riches with bounteous hand. Our King does not desire gold nor gems, but virtue, glory, immortality . . .' If there was another lesson to be learned about Henry from the smiling ease with which he had Empson and Dudley, his father's two tax-collectors-in-chief, tried and executed, it was lost in the public acclaim which greeted this sinister act. As the young King fulfilled the hopes and desires of the living, so did he those of his dead father by honouring Henry VII's dying request. Six weeks after the old King's death, he was married to Catherine of Aragon, to whom he had been betrothed since the age of twelve, at a private ceremony at the Chapel of the Franciscan Observants at Greenwich. Two weeks later on Midsummer's Day, the royal pair were crowned at Westminster at a ceremony of unsurpassed magnificence which served to underline the contrast between the new reign and that which twenty-four years earlier had founded the Tudor dynasty.

ELIZABETHA · VXOR
HENRICI · VII

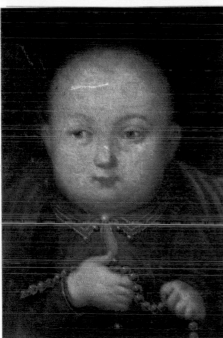

Above left
Elizabeth of York (1465-1503)
Henry was always fond of his wife
Elizabeth and was much affected by
her death. Nevertheless he married her
strictly for political reasons, and she
played little part in his life except as
the mother of his children. Despite the
dubious nature of his descent from John
of Gaunt, Henry regarded himself as the
representative of the Lancastrian line;
by his marriage to the daughter of
Edward IV he claimed therefore, that
he was uniting the Houses of Lancaster
and York, though he was careful not to
base his claim to the crown on the match.

Below left
Henry VIII as a child
By comparison with the childhood of his
father, the early years of Henry VIII were
calm and uneventful. Perhaps the main
reason for this was that Henry was not the
first son of the marriage of Henry VII and
Elizabeth of York. Until he was eleven,

Henry lived in the shade of his elder
brother, Prince Arthur. Although he
was Lord Lieutenant of Ireland and
Duke of York from an early age, it was
not until Arthur's death that he received
any particular attention. Not that the
deference and the flattering attention of
the court was allowed to interfere with
his education, supervised by his
grandmother, the Lady Margaret.

Above right
Margaret Beaufort (1443-1509)
While Henry VII had little time to
devote to cultural matters, his mother,
Margaret Beaufort, the Countess of
Richmond, devoted her life to the New
Learning of the Renaissance and to the
patronage of those men who were among
its leading figures. Over thirty years
before the beginning of her grandson's
reign she was supporting such men as
Caxton, while by her death, a few months
after that of Henry VII, the men she had
encouraged included More and Erasmus.

Henry VII Gateway, Windsor Castle
Although one of the major royal
residences that Henry VIII inherited
from his father, he did not spend much
time here during the early years of his
reign, for the royal apartments were
uncomfortable and not nearly so well-
appointed as those at Greenwich and
Richmond. Nevertheless Henry VII had
virtually completed the work begun in
Edward IV's day on the Chapel of St
George. With the completion of the
Chapel in 1519 and the restitution of
regular investiture ceremonies for the
Order of the Garter, other work at
Windsor was set afoot and the
gateway dates from this period.

Left

The Great Hall, Eltham Palace
Much of Henry's childhood was spent at
Eltham in Kent, together with his
brothers and sisters. This palace, set in
spacious grounds, was one of the
traditional royal residences. It had been
renovated by Henry VII who provided
the great hall with this hammerbeam roof.
Although the moat prevented much in the
way of enlargement, Henry soon added a
new bedchamber for Queen Catherine,
a study for himself and a new chapel.
The palace remained in regular use
throughout the reign.

Below

The Betrothal of Catherine and Arthur
Catherine finally arrived in England in the autumn of 1501, when she was fifteen, and this scene shows the young princess being presented to Prince Arthur. The marriage took place on 14th November, 1501. Although the fourteen year-old Arthur was a delicate boy, the young couple were despatched forthwith to Ludlow Castle to hold their court as Prince and Princess of Wales. Among their attendants was the young Charles Brandon who, a quarter of a century later, as Duke of Suffolk, was to testify that this marriage was consummated, claiming that Arthur had emerged from his wife's chamber on the morning after the wedding night saying, 'Last night I was in Spain—marriage is thirsty work'.

Right

Ferdinand and Isabella entering Granada (1492)
By his marriage to Isabella, Ferdinand had joined the two ancient kingdoms of Aragon and Castile. This was to be just the first stage in a life-long struggle to establish Spain as a unified European power. Determined and politically devious, Ferdinand exhibited many of the qualities Macchiavelli listed as necessary for a successful prince; but it was Isabella, fired by a burning religious fanaticism, who rallied the Catholic troops of Spain to the crusade against the Moors, who still held the southern kingdom of Granada. With the military crusade won, Isabella gave her attention to encourage the Inquisition in its sombre work.

Above

Desiderius Erasmus (1466-1536)
One of the greatest of the European
Renaissance scholars, Erasmus had many
connections with English men of letters.
Among these were such men as Thomas
More and Lord Mountjoy. It was on his
first visit to England at the turn of the
century that he was entertained by
Margaret Beaufort at Eltham, and first
saw the young Henry VIII, then aged
eight. One result of this meeting was the
poem *Prosopopaeia Britanniae*, dedicated
to Duke Henry. In 1509 with the
accession of Henry, he returned, and
although Henry lavished praise upon his
work, his hopes for the King's patronage
were not fulfilled, and he left England
somewhat disillusioned in July 1514.

Right

Margaret Tudor (1489-1541)
Henry VII's projects for dynastic alliances
did not only involve his sons. Anxious to
secure his northern borders he began
negotiations for the marriage of his
daughter Margaret to James IV of
Scotland in 1495. Despite James's
reluctance, the alliance was concluded in
1502 and sealed by the marriage in 1505.
Ten years later, Henry VIII's unruly
brother-in-law was to die at Flodden in
an unsuccessful attempt to invade
England and win the throne.

Far right

Henry VIII and His Father
This inkwash design by Holbein dates
from 1537, and was intended to form
part of the decoration of the palace of
Whitehall, which Henry had received from
Cardinal Wolsey. The theme, however, is
one which underlines much of
Henry VII's reign: through the pose and
bearing of his royal subject Holbein
created the aura of regal majesty which
all the Tudors were at pains to foster. At
the same time, the presence of Henry VII
in the background suggests that sense of
royal lineage which the old king did not
possess and yet struggled to provide for
his descendants.

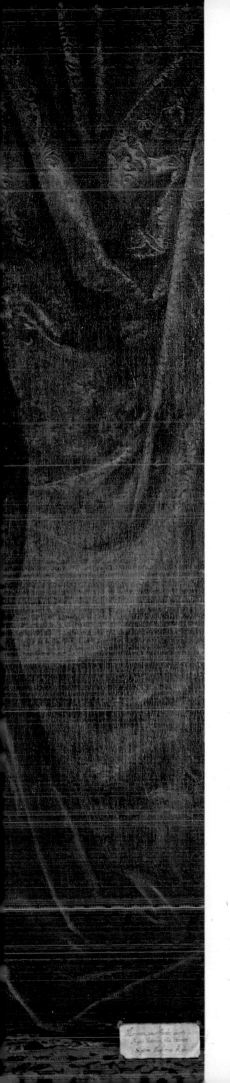

Catherine of Aragon

As the diplomatic marriages of the time went, this royal marriage began in the most auspicious circumstances. Both the King and Queen were young and personable and if Catherine was a few years older than Henry, her slight advantage in age only served to balance his youthful enthusiasm. More important than this, each was smitten with the other. A few months after the wedding Henry wrote to his father-in-law, Ferdinand, extolling the 'inestimable virtues' of his wife, 'which day by day do more and more shine forth, flourish and increase — so that even if we were still free it is she, nevertheless, whom we would choose for our wife before all others.' As for Catherine, she wrote at the same time to inform her father that she was 'so well married that no more can be said', and that she loved her new husband 'much more than herself'.

Catherine had special reason, if not to love her husband, then certainly to feel extremely grateful towards him, for it was Henry who by marrying her had lifted her out of seven years of misery and loneliness. Although she had been warmly and enthusiastically received on her arrival in England in 1501, her circumstances were soon to change drastically. Then she had been the bride-to-be of the heir to the throne, and subsequently his bride. Arthur's death in 1502, however, had thrown her back into the tangled world of international politics, and she had become a pawn in the interminable wrangling that went on

between Henry VII and her parents. It was soon apparent that both sides were in favour of marrying her to her young brother-in-law, but first the question of her virginity had to be settled to the satisfaction of all — a lengthy process involving an appeal to the Pope. The betrothal to Henry had taken place in 1503, but this had meant little to Catherine in her new life of penury and neglect, for it was well known that such contracts could easily be, and often were, annulled. In fact, to prevent any bond developing between the betrothed, Catherine was kept apart from Henry and saw little of him.

But with her marriage to Henry her poverty and material hardship were past. Profiting from the lavishness which characterized the court life at the beginning of the new reign, she was able to indulge the tastes she shared with her husband for all those activities which went to make his court one of the gayest in Europe. Of a more serious temperament than Henry (she had received an education in no way inferior to his and she enjoyed the company of learned men, to the delight of the aged Countess of Richmond), she nevertheless played with enthusiasm her part in the perpetual round of *bals masqués*, formal dances and musical entertainments which so delighted the King. Out of doors, she took part in the chase and was an enthusiastic spectator of the jousting displays and tournaments at which Henry delighted to show off his skill.

Far left

Henry VIII

During these early years Henry basked in general applause, not the least for his looks. A Venetian at the English court wrote home: 'His majesty is the handsomest potentate I ever set eyes on. Above the usual height, with an extremely fine calf to his leg, his complexion very fair and bright . . . and a round face so very beautiful that it would become a pretty woman.' This portrait, by an unknown artist, shows very clearly the family resemblance to his father and brother.

Left

Writing Desk

The magnificence of this writing desk is in keeping with the homage paid by Henry to the power of the written word at this time. Henry's arms are quartered with those of Catherine, and set between paintings of Venus and Mars. This was the period of much of Henry's own literary output although ironically he was somewhat lazy about the actual business of writing. Within a very short time of his accession he had made a stamp bearing his own signature which allowed him to escape the duty of signing his royal papers.

Right

Young Catherine of Aragon

When Henry VII came to inspect his daughter-in-law on the road to London in October 1501, he pronounced himself satisfied as to her ability to bear children. He was also impressed by her agreeable and dignified manners and by her pretty and well-rounded appearance. Catherine's attractiveness was in part a cause of her troubles during her years in the wilderness between 1502 and 1509. For Henry VII, although he had betrothed her to his second son, was not willing to commit himself actively to the Spanish alliance while more advantage was still to be gained from sitting on the fence.

In addition to being the King's companion, Catherine was also the Queen whose central role was to provide children to continue the royal line. In this respect she was a dutiful wife (and Henry an attentive husband) and the still-born child to which she gave birth seven months after her marriage was only the first in a long line of pregnancies. Within four months of this it was known that another child was on the way, and on New Year's Day, 1511, Catherine gave birth amid wild rejoicing to a baby son who was immediately named Henry, Prince of Wales, and acclaimed heir to the throne. Enormous sums of money were spent to celebrate his birth and continual festivity marked the first weeks of his life. Within two months, however, the baby prince was dead. Despite the disappointment of sickly infants and still-births, Henry did not despair; such mortality was in no way unusual for the time, and both he and his Queen were young enough to have many more children.

Catherine's major task then, was to provide an heir to the throne of England. Yet during those early years at least she herself remained very much a daughter of Spain. Despite the callous indifference shown by her father to her miserable situation during the years after the death of Prince Arthur, Catherine remained conscious of the reason which had brought her to England: that she was in fact an extension of her father's policy. As she saw it, this involved no conflict of loyalties; it was in Henry's interests to ally himself to Spain. Such an attitude was easy to hold since Henry shared it. As Catherine was able to report to Ferdinand early in the reign: 'I have performed the office of ambassador as Your Highness commanded, and as was known by the King My Lord, who places himself entirely in your hands.'

Ferdinand lost no time in exploiting his daughter's influence over Henry, and in his efforts to draw him into his struggle with France, he found the young King by no means unwilling to participate. For Henry, ironically enough in the light of later events, was the Pope's man (excessively so, according to Thomas More with whom the King was wont to discuss such matters) and he was well aware that the Papal States themselves were threatened by the might of the French armies in Italy. In any case, Macchiavelli had been right when he remarked that Henry was a Prince 'greedy for glory'.

In spite of, or perhaps because of, the object lesson in European politics provided by the expedition to Guienne in 1512, Henry equipped an army from his father's treasure and led it across the channel in 1513. Although his army did not win the renown of that of Henry V, it did well enough, capturing Thérouanne and Tournay, and carrying several minor skirmishes with the French, notably at the 'Battle of the Spurs'.

Before he left for France, Henry had underlined the confidence and trust he had in Catherine by appointing her regent of England. In addition, unsure of his northern frontier, he had left her in charge of all the armed forces in England. Henry had good reason to be uncertain of his Scottish brother-in-law,

James IV; no sooner had he left the country than the Scots King marched south with a huge army, far outnumbering the twenty thousand men posted in the north under the command of the aged Earl of Surrey. Catherine justified Henry's confidence to the full: she quickly rallied an enormous force from the south and despatched it northwards. Preparing to go north herself, she was stopped only by the news of Flodden.

But if Catherine had earned all Henry's trust, her father was soon to destroy her influence for good. No sooner had Henry returned from France in the winter of 1513 than Louis XII revealed to Henry that both Ferdinand and Maximilian had treated with him behind Henry's back. Henry's reaction was immediate: on the political front he replied to his former allies' treachery, to their intense dismay, by the political and diplomatic coup of marrying his sister Mary to the aged Louis; at home he turned against his wife as Ferdinand's representative at his court. Although Henry's displeasure with Catherine expressed itself merely in the dismissal of her Spanish confessor, the new French alliance meant in effect the end of her influence over Henry, and her political isolation at court.

The rift did not last long. In 1515 Louis XII died, to be succeeded by Francis I, thus bringing to an end the French alliance. In 1516 Catherine gave birth to a daughter, Mary. Although the child was a girl, its good health gave hope for future sons and Henry was delighted. Furthermore the death of Ferdinand in the same year, and the succession of Catherine's nephew, Charles V, made a Spanish alliance once more attractive. Nevertheless, although Catherine regained her place in Henry's affection, she did not regain her place in his councils. For by 1516 political preeminence after the King had shifted to Thomas Wolsey. The hope raised by Mary's birth was not to be fulfilled, and Catherine's only contribution to history, in the years before the divorce became a public debate, was her failure to provide Henry with a male heir to secure the succession.

Left, above and below
Scenes from the Great Tournament Roll of Westminster

This scene shows Henry jousting before Queen Catherine at the tournament held on 12th February, 1511, to celebrate the birth of the Prince of Wales. Jousting was a major expression of the cult of chivalry, which remained widespread in western Europe for much of the 16th century. It was of course completely spurious, but was a life-long passion of Henry. In 1536 a fall at the lists was to cause injuries to Henry's legs which developed later into the chronic ulcers that plagued his old age.

The second scene shows the royal Heralds on horseback summoning the challengers to the lists. Around the quartered arms of France and England, the fringes of the banners show the Tudor colours of green and white. One of the trumpeters is dark-skinned and may well have been a Moor from southern Spain. Despite the parochial nature of medieval Europe it appears that dark-skinned people from North Africa and perhaps beyond were not so uncommon a sight as may be supposed in Tudor England.

Above right
Henry walking to Parliament (1512)

Below right
The seating plan for the Blackfriars Parliament (1523)

The reign of Henry VIII was to see significant developments in the working of Parliament. In 1509 it was still largely an occasional body called primarily to provide money for the King's government. By Henry's death, after the turmoil of the Reformation, Parliament had become a more or less permanent institution and an integral part of the constitution. Far from being a body merely voting funds at the royal request, it now provided the legal instruments with which the king was able to enforce his will. Henry himself recognized this when he addressed Parliament in 1543: 'We at no time stand so highly in our estate royal as in the time of parliament.'

In contrast, the early Parliaments, like those of 1512 and 1523, were occupied solely in arguing about money. The seating plan of the latter shows what was already an out-of-date arrangement: within the court sits the king, with his Lords spiritual and temporal, while outside, at the bar, stand the Commons. Yet even before the revolution of 1530's, the Commons had already become the more important assembly attended by the King's ministers, although it was not until 1549 that they acquired a regular meeting place in St Stephen's Chapel at Westminster.

The Bataile of Spvrrs. anno. 1513.

Above

The Battle of the Spurs (August 1513)
This painting and that of **The Meeting between Henry VIII and Maximilian I** (*see pages 2-3*) record events during the campaigns of 1513. Henry arrived in France with a lavishly equipped army to discover that the French were not eager to fight. Brushing aside what little resistance there was, he pushed into French territory and laid seige to the fortified town of Thérouanne. Here he was joined by the Emperor Maximilian at the head of a large army; with much ceremony and regard for the niceties of precedence, the two monarchs

combined their forces to reduce the French town. When the French sent a force of cavalry to bring supplies to the beleaguered defenders, they were attacked by the Anglo-Imperial armies and beaten back. The engagement gained its name from the alacrity with which the French cavalry withdrew from the field. A few days later, when the town surrendered, Henry was enormously flattered by the deference of the Emperor, who begged him to be first to take possession of the captured prize. There was justice in this since it was Henry who had provided the funds to support his Imperial ally.

Pacteur.

Above
The Marriage of Mary Tudor and Louis XII

Right
Mary Tudor and Charles Brandon, Duke of Suffolk
One result of the war of 1513 that was unforeseen by the devious Ferdinand and his ally Maximilian was the marriage between Louis XII and Henry VIII's younger sister, the Princess Mary. This beautiful young girl was already in love with Charles Brandon, a close companion of the King. Nevertheless Mary was sent off to France to meet her husband to whom she had already been married by proxy, having previously renounced her long-standing betrothal to Charles of Castile (later the Emperor Charles V).

She was met by Louis at Abbeville in October, 1514. The aged lecher was beside himself with delight at his new young bride, and it was widely held that it was his feverish attempts to provide France with another royal baby that led to his death on New Year's Day, 1515, almost immediately after the marriage. Late in January, Brandon, who had been created Duke of Suffolk at the end of 1513, was sent to Cluny to bring the royal widow back to England after her period of mourning. Throwing caution to the winds, he married her instead. Although this runaway romance was not altogether unexpected, it was three months before the couple were allowed home.

Above
Giovanni de' Medici, Pope Leo X (1513-21)
The accession of Leo X in 1513 brought a change in Papal policy. Anxious to organize a crusade against the Turks who were pushing into south-eastern Europe, Leo tried to bring about a lasting peace in Europe. During the years before the Treaty of London in 1518, which was the culmination of this policy, Wolsey managed to extract a cardinal's hat from Leo X with the aid of an admiring Henry. In the year of the treaty he also gained a legate's commission from Leo.

Henry, too, extracted honours from this compliant Pope. In his case it was the addition to his royal style of *Fidei Defensor*, which was bestowed in October 1521.

Right
Cardinal Wolsey (1473?-1530)
From humble origins as the son of an Ipswich butcher, Wolsey had made for himself a steady career via Oxford and the Church, and after Henry VIII came to the throne, Wolsey was soon a member of the Council. The war of 1512-13 gave

him the opportunity to demonstrate his great talents, so that by 1515 he had ousted all other contenders for the King's confidence. He had an enormous appetite for preferment and office, both lay and ecclesiastic, and besides being legate and cardinal he soon held the Archbishopric of York, several other sees and deaneries, and the abbacy of St Albans. From Henry he received the Chancellorship. His inordinate love of pomp and display earned him the title of *alter rex* and characterized his fifteen-year domination of English politics and diplomacy.

21

CARDINAL   WOOLSE

Left
Henry VIII (L. Hornebolte)
Henry too was ageing and no longer presented the picture of triumphant youth; he was beginning to run to fat. He was able to carry this off, however, for his weight and build gave the impression of a strong and powerful monarch. Nevertheless he was still extremely vain about his appearance, and exhibited open jealousy when he heard reports of the good looks of Francis I, who had succeeded Louis XII in 1515. No longer visiting the Queen's bed, he was perpetually occupied with a string of mistresses, among whom Elizabeth Blount provided him with a son, to Catherine's bitter despair.

Opposite below left
Francis I (1494-1547) (attr. Clouet)
For over five years Henry basked in the adulation that Europe naturally accorded its royal *jeune premier* until the accession of Francis. The young French king, as eager for glory as Henry, underlined this challenge with the resounding victory of Marignano which gave him control in north Italy. Not content with military renown, Francis also set about creating an image of the Renaissance Prince by attracting to his court artists and scholars from all over Europe. Not unnaturally Henry was more than a little jealous and always immensely pleased to hear Francis compared unfavourably with himself.

The European scene was dominated during these years by the grandiose diplomacy which arose out of the rivalry existing between those three *jeunes premiers*, Charles V, Francis I, and Henry VIII; England's contribution, moreover, was further complicated by the efforts of Cardinal Wolsey to have himself elected pope. Nevertheless, Henry's (and therefore Wolsey's) attention was more and more taken up by the problem of the succession. At first, this preoccupation manifested itself in moves to complete his father's policy of eliminating possible rivals to the Tudor line. In 1521 Edward Stafford, Duke of Buckingham, was suddenly brought to trial, condemned and executed for high treason. He was not the first such victim of Henry VIII's reign; in 1513 Edmund de la Pole had been executed for his descent from the Yorkist Kings, but there had been definite proof of treasonable activity on his part while Buckingham was the victim solely of the King's anxiety at the absence of an heir.

In 1517, desperate to find some positive solution to the problem of the succession the King took the step of advancing Henry Fitzroy, his natural son by Elizabeth Blount, who was in his sixth year, to the ranks of Duke of Richmond and Earl of Nottingham and Somerset, although he must have been aware of the danger to the succession if this boy should ever come to the throne for bastards were held in as little regard as women. Significantly he was placed before the whole of the nobility in rank and was even given precedence at court over the Princess Mary. Shortly afterwards Mary herself was sent from court to take up residence at Ludlow Castle.

Despite these honours Henry realized that such a policy was ultimately unsatisfactory, and it was at about this time that the old question of the validity of his marriage to Catherine was reopened. The problem was twofold: first, was Catherine a virgin at Arthur's death, and secondly, did the Pope have the right to grant a dispensation for the marriage to Henry? The first point rested on a matter of evidence: Catherine claimed that she was still a virgin in 1509, Arthur had boasted to the contrary. The second point was a theological one: the case against the marriage resting on a passage from Leviticus, the case for upon a passage from Deuteronomy. Whatever the truth of the matter, the string of miscarriages and still-births made it evident to the men of the time that God had not favoured the marriage. Catherine saw these sad events as a Divine punishment for the death of the Earl of Warwick, which was a prerequisite of her arrival in England. Henry however, believed, or had convinced himself that the punishment was for having lived in sin outside the bonds of true marriage.

The matter was handed to Wolsey; as he was a Cardinal and Papal Legate in England, he was instructed by Henry to produce, with the utmost discretion, a case for annulling the King's marriage. By 1527, there was another element: Henry's desire to marry Anne Boleyn, with whom he had secretly fallen in love.

When the question was first discussed by Henry and Wolsey there seemed to be no major problem to its solution; there were many precedents among the royal houses of Europe for such a course of action, and Henry, as a faithful son of the Church, had every reason to hope for the Pope's willing cooperation in the matter. It was decided that Wolsey and Archbishop Warham should summon Henry to appear before them to answer a charge of living in sin with Catherine. This charge was to be proved despite Henry's feigned protests and the case presented to the Pope with the subsequent judgment being 'forced' on the King. In May 1527 the meetings began to be reported to Catherine, who at first refused to believe in Henry's complicity,

Right
Catherine of Aragon in middle age
Henry's devoted love for Catherine did
not long survive her final miscarriage in
1518. The six-year difference in their ages
was now noticeable: in any case the
continual string of miscarriages that
Catherine had suffered had not dealt
kindly with her looks. By the 1520's she
was ageing fast, putting on weight around
the face and body, and generally
beginning to look the middle-aged matron.
When Henry and Catherine visited France
together, Francis expressed the opinion:
'The King of England is young — but his
wife is old and deformed.'

Below right
**The Embarkation of Henry for the Field
of the Cloth of Gold (1520)**
Accustomed as the premier port of the
kingdom was to the comings and goings
of royalty, Dover had never seen anything
like the splendour of Henry leaving the
harbour with his train of over five
thousand people and their equipment.
The upheaval was the more marked by the
presence of the newly-elected Emperor,
Charles V. His talks with Henry and their
agreement to meet again after Henry's
interview with Francis raised French
suspicions and emphasized rightly the
essential pointlessness of the Anglo-
French meeting.

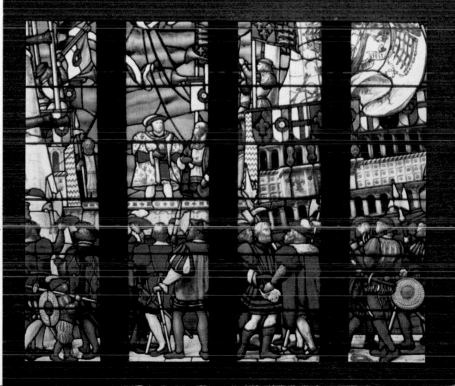

preferring to blame Wolsey; but although she pretended ignorance of the proceedings she nevertheless informed her nephew, Charles V. His troops sacked Rome in the same month.

Pope Clement was now Charles' prisoner and in no position to grant Henry's demand. Although he valued Henry's faithful support, and although he feared for the English Church, he was more impressed by the threat posed by Charles V who made it clear that he would not tolerate the annulment of his aunt's marriage.

A series of French victories in this year led to a temporary amelioration in the situation, and Clement apparently relented to the extent of sending Cardinal Campeggio to England armed with a commission to deal with the matter. In fact Campeggio had been told to delay as much as possible in the hope that the problem would resolve itself, to try to arrange a settlement out of court, but on no account to give a decision. He finally arrived in England in October, trying first to persuade Catherine with the help of Wolsey and Henry, to concede defeat and enter a nunnery where she would be treated with all deference and honour even to the extent of having charge of her daughter. Catherine refused point blank to consider such a proposal. In the end he was forced to bring the matter to trial in June 1529. The court opened at Blackfriars presided over by Wolsey and Campeggio. Although both Henry and Catherine were present, Catherine stayed only to make an impassioned plea in defence of her case on her knees before the King, and then left the court. The proceedings went on in her absence, marked only by the unexpected opposition to the King's case of John Fisher, the aged Bishop of Rochester. Apart from this interlude the events of the trial were predictable. The final day arrived on 23rd July, and Henry returned to the court to watch events from the gallery. In the meanwhile Campeggio had made in private a

final but unsuccessful appeal to Catherine. Convinced of the King's determination he realized he could no longer delay a final decision. To the shocked surprise of the King, he referred the matter to Rome.

This decision led in November of that year to the summoning of what is known to history as the Reformation Parliament. Despite the significance of these public events in which Catherine took no part, she continued to be seen with the King on state occasions and to see him less publicly at court until mid-1531. Change was nigh however, for Henry had been developing the palaces of Hampton Court and Whitehall which he had received from a Wolsey desperate to regain the King's favour after the failure of the Blackfriars trial. Henry intended these places and particularly the latter as residences for himself and Anne Boleyn, and had made no provision for the Queen. On 11th July the King left Windsor on a hunting trip with Anne Boleyn never to see Catherine again. By the time he returned she had been ordered to remove to the More (yet another of Wolsey's properties) forbidden either to write to Henry, or to see her daughter.

Early in the next year Anne Boleyn was established in the Queen's apartments at court, while Catherine was removed to a succession of ever-more distant royal manors, until she finally arrived at Kimbolton in Huntingdonshire. Here she stayed until her death in January 1536, having spent the years in between in total political isolation. Her last act was to dictate from her deathbed a letter to Henry in which she pleaded with him to consider the salvation of his soul, and to be merciful to their daughter Mary. She also asked for pensions and dowries for the few who remained in her household.

'Lastly', she wrote, 'I make this vow, that mine eyes desire you above all things. Farewell.'

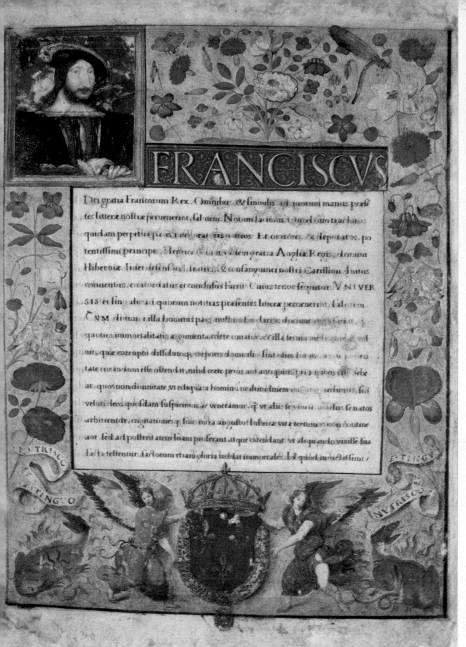

Previous pages
The Field of the Cloth of Gold (1520)
Despite the fact that political events were
moving England towards an alliance with
Spain against France, this meeting
between Francis and Henry was a display
of unparalleled magnificence and
pageantry. Since the castle at Guisnes,
where the meeting was to take place, was
considered unsuitable for a royal lodging,
a whole new town of tents and pavilions
was set up to house the vast numbers of
people involved. Inevitably the political
discussions between Francis and Henry
took a back seat, while most of the time
was devoted to chivalric competition
on the field and in the lists. The whole
episode was symbolized by the event
which was to end the festivities. Cardinal
Wolsey laid the foundation stone of a
chapel dedicated to Our Lady of
Friendship, to be jointly built and
maintained by the Kings of England and
France. It was never built.

Above left
**Title Page of the Ratification of the Treaty
of Westminster made at Amiens on
18 August, 1527**
By 1527 the anti-French policy of the
Emperor had pushed Francis towards an
understanding with the English, and
Wolsey saw the treaty of 'perpetual
peace' signed in April. The imposing
nature of the document, bearing Francis'
portrait and his personal emblem, the
salamander, did not disguise the
worthlessness of the treaty and the
ultimate futility of Wolsey's foreign
policy. Francis continued to treat with
Charles V and the separate peace
concluded at Cambrai in 1529 between
France and Spain ended Wolsey's vain
interventions in European affairs.

Above right
**Giulio de' Medici, Pope Clement VII
(1523-34)**
The sack of Rome in 1527 and the
quasi-captivity into which Clement fell
necessarily changed the goodwill hitherto
shown to the Tudors, despite Wolsey's
desperate efforts. When Clement
regularized his position *vis-à-vis* the
Emperor by the Treaty of Barcelona in
1529, he inevitably pushed the English
Church into schism. By the time that he
issued the sentence of excommunication
on Henry in September 1533, the King
had already turned his back on the Pope.

Right
Charles V (1500-58) (Titian)
While Henry and Francis were both
extrovert glory-seekers who revelled in
the wealth and trappings of power, the
succession of Charles V to the throne of
Castile in 1516, and his election to the
Imperial throne in 1519, brought to the
European stage an entirely different sort
of Prince. A stolid, melancholic man who
displayed no sign of the overt enjoyment
of rule, he created none of the aura that
his brother princes were so careful to
maintain. Indeed, he finally renounced his
crowns and title and retired at the end of
his life to a monastery in Estremadura.

Left

John Fisher, Bishop of Rochester (1461-1535)

While Warham was compliant to the King's wishes, John Fisher was not. Although Henry let pass his opposition during the trial at Blackfriars in 1529, Fisher could not escape the requirement that he take the oath supporting the Act of Succession. Since the preamble asserted the religious supremacy of the King and denied the authority of the Pope, this oath was unacceptable to Fisher; for his defiance he was executed on 23rd June 1535.

Right

Archbishop Warham (1457-1532)

Wolsey was not the only cleric engaged in the King's 'Great Matter' during the early years; there was also William Warham, the Archbishop of Canterbury. He was already an old man of seventy when called upon by Henry to try his case with Wolsey; indeed, it was longevity in office that frustrated Wolsey's plans to don the primate's mitre. When Warham did die it was to make way for Thomas Cranmer. Warham was no martyr, and in his eagerness to smooth the King's path, he forged the signature of John Fisher on the document by which the English bishops declared their doubts concerning the King's marriage to Catherine of Aragon.

Below left

Cardinal Wolsey surrendering the Great Seal (1529)

With the failure of the Blackfriars trial, Wolsey was cast off by the King, his only support. Faced with many charges and stripped of most of his wealth and offices, he was forced to give up the Great Seal to the Dukes of Norfolk and Suffolk in October 1529. Shortly afterwards the new men banished him to his see of York, which he had never visited. He sent pleas to Charles and Francis, asking them to intercede with Henry on his behalf, which gave his restless enemies the opportunity to convince the King of his treason and he was arrested. On his way south to certain execution, he died at Leicester on 24th November 1530.

Above
Tom Quadrangle, Christchurch, Oxford
Wolsey's ambitions spread to the field of scholarship, and though no friend of the New Learning (he had organized the burning of books) he had founded colleges at Ipswich and Oxford. The latter was endowed in 1525 and named Cardinal's College, but it remained unfinished upon his death. Henry took over the task of completion, renaming the college Christchurch. Despite the pious name, the cloisters which Wolsey had begun were never completed as Henry appropriated the funds. In any case the Dissolution of the Monasteries rendered them unnecessary.

Below left
Maximilian and Ferdinand after their investiture in the Order of the Garter
These pictures come from a working book of arms of the early 16th century. They show Maximilian, King of the Romans, and the Archduke Ferdinand, brother of Charles V, feasting after being invested with the insignia of the Order of the Garter. Both Henry VII and Henry VIII were eager that the Order of the Garter should carry great prestige, as was witnessed by the attention they devoted to St George's Chapel, Windsor. Just as

their European brethren distributed the ancient orders of chivalry to those they wished to favour whether they were worthy or no, so did the early Tudor monarchs with the Garter.

Below right
Catherine of Aragon a few years before her death (attr. L. Hornebolte)
Although Catherine died only a few weeks after her fiftieth birthday, she was already an old woman, aged not only by the physical trials she had suffered, but also by the sorrow of exile. Her death at Kimbolton Castle, near Peterborough, was followed by the usual crop of rumours that she had been poisoned, but there is no reason to believe that this was so. The conditions in the succession of royal manors to which she was condemned, plus the presence of her doctors, are themselves sufficient explanation of an early and sudden death.

Right
The Chapel Royal, Hampton Court
Henry's conventional piety and the emphasis he placed on regular attendance at the mass made the chapel an integral part of any royal palace. Not unnaturally

therefore, the Chapel at Hampton Court Palace was the object of Henry's special attentions in the years after 1525. At first Wolsey's original work was continued and the building completed. During 1535 and 1536, the business of decorating the Chapel was carried out. The crowning glory of this work was the beautiful ornate vaulted roof. With its gilded pendants and blue-starred vaulting, it provided a fitting setting for one of Henry's lifelong passions, the royal choir.

Following pages
Wolsey's closet at Hampton Court
Wolsey's craving for pomp and ceremony was reflected in the residences that he created for himself, several of which were scattered about the Home Counties. The splendour of Hampton Court was such that many were convinced that Wolsey was deliberately trying to outshine the King; certainly his patronage of the best in foreign craftsmen and artists equalled Henry's, as may be seen from the decorations of his private closet. Evidently Wolsey realized he had overreached himself, for in June 1525 he presented the Palace to the King, who accepted with alacrity and promptly set about adding to it.

Anne Boleyn

As a faithful daughter of the Catholic Church, Catherine had had good reason to be concerned for the state of Henry's soul. In his efforts to secure the succession he had led the English Church into open breach with Rome, he had flouted Papal authority in England and despite his own orthodoxy he had promoted both the men and the situation which were to lead to the overthrow of the old religion. Because of this Henry was under the threat of excommunication, and the Pope was later to call on all Christians to unite in ridding Christendom of such a heretic. Nevertheless, Catherine's deathbed plea fell on deaf ears, for Henry had long since confounded his political with his spiritual needs. Indeed, he was relieved by the news of her death since one more obstacle had been removed from his path.

From now on the politics of the breach with Rome were to transcend the divorce which had been its root cause. Yet in the decade preceding Catherine's death they had been dominated by the woman who had supplanted her as Queen, for whom Henry had set out to defy the Pope and the rest of Europe, and to destroy the power of the Church in England. That woman was Anne Boleyn.

The Boleyn family was of humble origin and had been occupied in commerce during the earlier part of the fifteenth century. Like other families of the period they had invested their wealth in land, using the position they gained thereby to enhance their social standing by marrying into the nobility. Sir Thomas Boleyn, Anne's father, had himself married Elizabeth Howard, daughter of the second Duke of Norfolk, the victor of Flodden, and had been employed in various offices at court. Both his daughters were educated in France and were judged by contemporary writers to be more French than English. When Mary, the elder one, came home early in the 1520's, she at once caught the King's eye and was soon his mistress. A year or so later when war threatened between France and England, Anne came back to the English court where she too attracted much attention though not immediately from the King. Among her admirers was the poet, Sir Thomas Wyatt, although Anne herself appears to have fallen in love with Lord Henry Percy, the son of the Earl of Northumberland. However, towards the end of 1525 or some time during 1526, Henry became tired of Mary and fell passionately in love with Anne, which may explain the energy

Left

Henry VIII (Joos van Cleve)
Courage was a quality that was needed to deal with a lover such as Henry. Twenty years of rule had somewhat tarnished the reputation for generous enthusiasm and youthful innocence that had so enchanted Erasmus. Nevertheless Henry in his prime still attracted the admiration of the world, as this extract from a letter written in 1531 by a Venetian ambassador illustrates: 'Never have I seen a man so handsome, elegant, and well-proportioned, as this English King; tall, agile, strong, with flesh all pink and white, graceful in his mein and his walk. It seems to me that Nature, in creating such a Prince, has done her utmost to present a model of manly beauty to these modern days.'

Right

Anne Boleyn (1502?-36) (attr. Holbein)
As a result of Henry's passion Anne Boleyn found herself at the centre of a religious and political revolution which aroused the strongest feelings; not unnaturally, much of what has been written about her has been coloured by these emotions. However the quality that brought Anne to the stage of history was courage and this was recognized even by her enemies: Eustace Chapuys, the Imperial ambassador, paid tribute to it when he wrote home 'This lady is braver than a Lion'. Thomas Wyatt, who was smitten with love yet knew she was unattainable, wrote:
'There is written her fair neck round about
Noli me tangere, for Caesar's I am
And wild for to hold, though I seem tame.'

with which Wolsey had broken up her affair with the young Lord Percy.

Because of the central role she played in the history of these years, Anne Boleyn has received much attention from writers of polemic of both sides of the religious divide. Many descriptions of her are therefore distorted by prejudice. Those who supported Catherine related stories of hideous deformities, while their opponents were given to lyrical eulogizing on her beauty. In fact she appears to have merited neither treatment, and perhaps an Italian account written in 1532 when she was about twenty-six years of age presents a more likely picture: 'Madame Anne is not one of the handsomest women in the world. She is of middling stature, swarthy complexion, long neck, wide mouth, not a very full bosom, and in fact has nothing but the passion of the King and her eyes which are black and beautiful, and have a great effect.'

Whatever her looks, they clothed a character of determination and cool nerve, for Anne resolved to accept Henry's suit only upon her own terms. Whether she set her sights upon the throne from the start is not certain, but faced with the example of her sister's fate, Anne refused to give in to Henry's advances.

Once Henry was aware of this, he determined to make her his wife and the mother of his heirs. With this desire came the realization that he would have not only to free himself from the bonds of the Spanish marriage but also endeavour to prove it invalid. This decision had a marked effect upon the lady. Assured of her position in the King's affections, and of his intentions, and aided by the group of leading courtiers led by her father and the Dukes of Norfolk and Suffolk, Anne began to press Henry forward. Nevertheless the years passed in fruitless attempts to coerce the Pope to a favourable decision in the matter of the validity of Henry's marriage to Catherine.

With the resignation of More in 1532 there emerged a new man who was to dominate the political scene throughout the decade: Thomas Cromwell. That he brought with him a new approach to the question is evident from the fact that on 1st September 1532 Henry felt confident enough to create Anne Marquess of Pembroke and openly to give her preeminence both at home and abroad. Shortly afterwards she accompanied Henry to Boulogne to meet Francis I, where she was shown the deference normally reserved for a Queen. This was a notable advance, for until that time Henry had been very circumspect about being seen in public with Anne in view of the hostility aroused in the country and abroad by his treatment of Catherine.

This development may well have occurred as a celebration of the consummation of their love, for by January 1533 it was evident that Anne was pregnant, which speeded up the plans already laid. On 25th January, Henry and Anne were secretly married. Six weeks later Parliament passed the Act in Restraint of Appeals to Rome, the legal instrument with which Henry was to settle the question of his marriage once and for all. Towards the end of March, Thomas Cranmer, one of the King's new men, was canonically consecrated Archbishop of Canterbury in succession to Warham who had died in the previous August. Scarcely consecrated, Cranmer presided over the court held at Dunstable in May to decide the issue of the marriage which had been removed from the Pope's hands by the Act of Appeals. Naturally the verdict issued on 23rd May was in Henry's favour. One week later on 1st June Anne Boleyn processed with lavish pomp from the Tower of London to Westminster to be crowned Queen of England. It only remained in the following year to round off the process begun by the Act of Appeals with the Acts of Succession and Supremacy, which were to claim so many victims, among whom were Thomas More and John Fisher. By this time however, the fortunes of Anne Boleyn herself were on the downward slope, for Henry's great love did not long survive the royal honeymoon.

The first mistake that Anne Boleyn made was on 7th September 1533, when she gave birth to a daughter, Elizabeth. Although Henry took hope from the fact that the child was healthy, he was disappointed, and did not trouble to conceal it. After six years of devoted attention, the new Queen was soon facing the indignity of royal mistresses. In 1534 she once again appeared to be pregnant, though this turned out to be a false alarm, and Henry turned back to his mistress, herself a cousin of the Boleyns. The final blow came in January 1536 on the day that Catherine of Aragon was buried. In the fourth month of her third pregnancy Anne miscarried a baby boy. In vain did she protest to the furious Henry that her miscarriage had been brought on by the news of an accident that he had had while at the lists; it was not to be long before he rid himself of her.

A mere two months or so after this event an investigation into the conduct of the Queen was begun by the Privy Council. Those responsible concentrated their attention on collecting information about the young men who had attached themselves to the Queen's court. It did not appear to be a question so much of collecting evidence — none was ever produced — but of building up a credible case against the Queen. This the Council did, naming five men; three were from the royal household (Brereton, Norris and Weston), the fourth was Anne's own brother, Lord Rochford and the fifth was Smeaton, a court musician. Under torture, or the threat thereof, two of these men, Norris and Smeaton, admitted adultery with the Queen. A few days later at the beginning of May Anne herself was summoned before the Council at Greenwich. The hearing was held in secret, and as a result Anne was committed to the Tower. Two weeks later, armed with the convictions of the five men, the special commission charged with the case tried Anne herself and condemned her to death. On 19th May, she was beheaded by the French swordsman brought over from St Omer especially for the purpose. She died protesting her innocence, and declaring her devotion to her 'most gentle Sovereign Lord', the King.

37

Left

Mary Boleyn (1503?-?) (attr. Holbein)
Despite Henry's dashing good looks, his lover Anne would not go to his bed. This may have been partly from ambition, but Anne also had the fate of her sister Mary before her. Having given in to the King's advances, Mary was then cast off and her husband William Carey was obliged by the King to send her away from court. When William died in 1528 from the sweating sickness Mary was destitute, and lived with her father only through the good offices of her sister. Six years later, Mary married Sir William Stafford (a man of little fortune and less position). They were married without the King's consent, and his disapproval of the match condemned her to a life of obscure poverty.

Right

Sir Thomas Boleyn, Viscount Rochford and Earl of Wiltshire (1477-1539)
(Holbein)
One man who reaped enormous profit from the King's attentions to the Boleyn girls was their father, Thomas. Even his early advancement in the King's service was probably due to a liaison between his wife, Elizabeth Howard, and Henry. When Mary had caught the King's eye, he received his peerage (1525), and then during Anne's dominance he quickly advanced to the highest rank, receiving the Garter and becoming Lord Privy Seal and a leading member of the King's Council. Nevertheless, his affection for his children lasted only as long as they were useful to him; only with reluctance did he eventually agree to take back his daughter, Mary, and then at the express command of the King. Skilful at preserving his own life, he continued to hold high office after the execution of his children, Anne and George, and expressed no hint of protest or sorrow at their death.

Above
Detail from the rood screen of King's College Chapel, Cambridge
Although Henry VII had left £10,000 in his will towards the completion of King's College Chapel, it was not until 1532 that his son made a grant of money to provide for the interior decoration of the building. In that year however, work was started on the magnificent rood screen and organ loft which now grace the chapel. In honour of the King's pious generosity the screen is liberally decorated with his initials and those of Anne Boleyn, who was to become Queen in the year that the work was completed. The college also owes much of its stained glass to Henry VIII's patronage.

Top
Beckley Manor, Otmoor, Oxfordshire
This manor was built as a hunting lodge during the early 16th century. Henry possessed several such lodges scattered around the Home Counties to which he used to repair with a select band of intimates on his frequent hunting trips. Henry had always been a passionate huntsman; so much so that, according to one of his secretaries, Richard Pace, he had turned the sport into a 'Royal martyrdom'. The arrival of Anne Boleyn only encouraged him further although Catherine had also been keen. For Anne, the hunting trip provided an opportunity to get the King away from court and thus from the Queen. Indeed, it was to go on such a trip that Henry bade goodbye for the last time to Catherine in 1531.

Above right
Anne Boleyn's Gateway, Hampton Court
Henry's courtship and marriage with Anne Boleyn occurred while the work at Hampton Court was in progress. It was only to be expected then that he should leave some memorial to his *grand amour*, although much has been obliterated by Anne's dramatic fall from grace. At one level this desire expressed itself in the linked initials of the royal couple carved in the panelling (Catherine's 'C' having been carefully but imperfectly erased to make way for her successor's 'A'). The gateway in the picture, which was embellished by Henry during the early 1530's, and which bears his royal arms,

was one more example; Henry named the gate after his Queen. Despite the disgrace and fall of Anne Boleyn the gate has retained her name.

Right
The Royal Lock
This lock, decorated with the royal arms and the Tudor rose, is a reminder of the fact that, though the rule of the Tudors marked a new era, there was much about their rule that was essentially medieval. While Westminster and the capital were becoming more and more the fixed centres of national life, the King himself was always on the move about the kingdom, as had been the case throughout the Middle Ages. Where the King went, there too went the court with all its paraphernalia. The lock was part of this peripatetic existence; it was removable and was fixed on the door of the royal bedroom of whichever residence the King chanced to stop at.

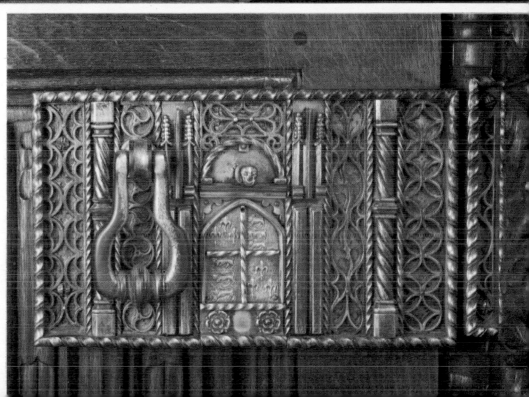

Far left
Designs for jewelry (Holbein)
Jewelry was far more important to the
people of Tudor England than it is today
and in a much more real sense. To invest
in jewelry was to invest in a highly
compact form of wealth: Henry VII
between the years 1491 and 1505 spent
£100,000 solely upon this form of wealth.
There was also another, social side to the
possession, and wearing, of jewelry. That
the nobility were highly conscious of the
status it represented may be inferred from
the number of laws forbidding the
non-noble wealthy from wearing many
forms of jewelry. Not unnaturally
Holbein was very interested in this form
of art. Quite apart from the considerable
number of separate drawings he did of
jewelry worn by members of the court,
it is always reproduced in great detail in
the portraits he painted.

Above left
Anne Boleyn's Bed

Below left
Anne Boleyn's Lute

Right
**Facsimile of the Clock presented by Henry
VIII to Anne Boleyn on their marriage**
All these items have been collected
together at Hever Castle, which was the
home of the Boleyn (or Bullen, the English
form of their name) family.

The bed-head is chiefly remarkable for
its size and ornate decoration. The idea of
the bed as something more than a mobile
couch which was removed during the day
to make way for day-time activities did
not become current in England until the
middle years of the century. Obviously
Anne Boleyn, as first lady of the kingdom,
would be likely to be an early recipient
of such modern notions.

The silver clock is of 16th-century
manufacture, and is a copy of the clock
presented by Henry VIII to Anne Boleyn
on the occasion of their marriage. It is
decorated with the royal coat of arms.

The nine-stringed lute is reputed to
have belonged to Anne Boleyn; it is resting
on a carved chest, probably made to
celebrate the elevation to the peerage in
1525 of her father. The instrument is an
example of very fine craftsmanship as
befitted a woman of her standing.
Nevertheless, her possession of such an
instrument merely reflected, as did the
King's passion for music, a national
preoccupation that lasted throughout the
century. Music was played by all levels
of society. Indeed, it is on record that
the barber surgeons of the Tudor period
used to keep a supply of musical
instruments to provide for the amusement
of their clients as they waited for
treatment.

Tho: Wiatt Knight.

Left
Westminster Hall
The oldest of the royal palaces that Henry VIII inherited was that of Westminster, which by the 16th century had become the centre of the monarchy. Not surprisingly, it was the scene of many of the great events of Henry's reign, despite the Great Fire of 1512. Having been married in the greatest secrecy, Anne was promised a magnificent coronation; the ceremony itself took place in the Abbey after a triumphal procession through London; a sumptuous banquet followed at Westminster Hall, with the Queen presiding. Three years later, however, the scene of her triumph was to witness Anne's downfall; in May 1536 the commission led by her uncle Norfolk, having examined her at Greenwich, now judged her guilty at a trial held in the Hall at Westminster.

Right
Sir Thomas More (1478-1535)
(after Holbein)
Perhaps one of the greatest Englishmen of Tudor England was Sir Thomas More. An exponent of the New Learning of the Renaissance, he was the author of *Utopia* and the friend of Erasmus. More was also the King's friend, although he had no illusions as to the depth of that friendship, and he served Henry in various posts, including, during the years 1529-1532, that of Lord Chancellor. In this capacity he directed Henry's efforts in Parliament to secure the divorce. More was essentially a man of the medieval world and, unhappy at the trend of events, he retired from public life. Rather than deny the final authority of the Pope, he went to the scaffold, one of the early martyrs of the nation state.

Below left
Sir Thomas Wyatt (1503?-42) (Holbein)
Best known for his love for Anne Boleyn and for the poems he wrote on this subject (which were not published until very much later) Thomas Wyatt was the man who introduced the Petrarchan sonnet into English poetry. As a young knight in the King's service he had spent much time in Italy, and had discovered new poetic forms that his younger friend, the Earl of Surrey, was to develop. Wyatt's accomplishment brought him early to Henry's attention, and he was a leading courtier, despite his frequent visits to the European courts. His devotion to Anne Boleyn almost cost him his life, and he was imprisoned in 1536 but released for lack of evidence.

Jane Seymour

Henry had good reason for getting rid of Anne Boleyn; since the previous autumn he had been in love with Jane Seymour, whom he was determined to marry. With admirable timing he was betrothed to this lady on the day after Anne's execution and married her ten days later on 30th May.

The new Queen came from an old-established landed family from Wiltshire. Her father was Sir John Seymour, an old servant of Henry who had fought alongside him in France in 1513, and who had formed part of his train at the Field of the Cloth of Gold. Her mother was a member of the Wentworth family and was consequently descended from Edward III. Although the father had long since retired to his lands, his eldest son Edward was rapidly rising to a position of influence in court circles. His career had started with service as a page in Mary Tudor's household when she was Queen of France. Upon his return to England he entered Wolsey's service, eventually accompanying Henry and Anne Boleyn to Boulogne in 1532. It was probably this experience that persuaded Seymour where his own and his family's interests lay. Shortly after this his sister Jane left the post she held as lady-in-waiting to Queen Catherine, and joined the service of Anne Boleyn. Not that Jane came immediately to Henry's attention; it was a year or so before he stayed at Wolf Hall, their family home, during the course of his autumn progress in 1533. Whether or not this visit was the occasion or the result of his noticing Jane is unknown.

At first Henry can have courted Jane only as a prospective mistress, yet shortly after the visit to Wolf Hall, Anne miscarried and was doomed. Immediately the King was engaged in discussions with Cranmer and Cromwell as to the means of ridding himself of this Queen who could not provide him with an heir. At the same time, his overtures to Jane Seymour met with a rebuff. Well-schooled by her brother Edward, who had already been promoted for her sake to the Privy Chamber, Jane returned unopened the King's letter and a purse of sovereigns with the message that she was a virtuous maiden and could not accept such a gift unless 'God should send her some good and honest husband'. Such protestations of virtue on her part were no doubt sincere, for Jane had the reputation of being something of a prude. But the meaning of this incident was clear and the King was duly impressed. Shortly afterwards Cromwell was moved from his rooms at Greenwich so that Edward Seymour and his wife might move in. This was arranged to allow Henry to fulfil his promise not to see the lady 'except in the presence of one of her relatives'. Another indication of the way Henry's

Left

Henry VIII (Holbein)
It was the accident in the lists in 1536 that marked the turning-point in Henry's health. This fall was serious enough to prevent him from ever again taking part in the jousting and the athletic activities he had so loved as a young man. Always inclined to fat, the consequent reduction in his physical activity led inevitably to the obesity which characterizes his portraits from this time. The possibilities of this situation were not lost on the court; in 1537 Lord Montague was already writing that, 'He will die one day suddenly, his leg will kill him and then we shall have jolly stirring!'

Right

Jane Seymour (1512-37)
Jane Seymour is the wife about whom least is known. She appears to have been something of a cypher, used by her brother to advance the family interests and her personal motto, 'Bound to obey and serve', is an apt one, that contrasts sharply with Anne Boleyn's, 'The Happiest of Women'. A glance at this portrait of her seems to indicate that the match with Henry was hardly one based on passion. Nevertheless, her success in bearing a son secured her a place in his affections, and Henry chose to be buried with her in St George's Chapel at Windsor.

mind was working lay in the elevation to the Order of the Garter of Seymour's friend, Sir Nicholas Carew, over the head of Viscount Rochford, Anne Boleyn's brother.

It could not have been for her looks alone that Henry chose Jane as his next Queen. As Chapuys, the Imperial ambassador, wrote in a report to his master, 'Nobody thinks that she has much beauty. Her complexion is so fair that she may be called rather pale.' At this time Jane was about twenty-five years of age, and Chapuys went on to express his doubts about the virtue of one who had been 'so long at court', a significant comment upon the moral level to which Henry's court had sunk over the quarter century of his reign. What commended the new Queen to Henry was her healthy appearance and buxon figure, which contrasted with Anne's slimness. Moreover, she had many sisters, and, more important, brothers who had survived infancy: she was, then, of good breeding stock.

One small issue remained to be settled in order that their marriage should follow quickly and quietly upon the death of Anne Boleyn. This problem was dealt with by Cranmer who, as Primate of the newly independent Church, was able to grant the royal couple a dispensation allowing them to marry despite their consanguinity of the third degree. This was done on the day Anne Boleyn was executed. Although the betrothal and marriage (in the Queen's Chapel at Whitehall) took place as planned, Jane was never crowned Queen. The date for her Coronation was set for October, but had to be postponed because of the plague, and in the end never took place at all because of Jane's premature death.

The marriage was accompanied by a general reshuffle of the royal appointments as the Seymour interest was advanced: Edward became Viscount Beauchamp, while his friends occupied the posts left vacant by the deaths of Norris, Weston and Brereton. Nevertheless, the Queen's household remained little changed, for Jane herself was of a shy and quiet disposition, showing no inclination for court affairs. Apart from fulfilling her principal task of providing the King with an heir, Jane's major contribution was to help bring about the reconciliation between Henry and his elder daughter Mary, who had for so long refused to recognize the fact of her own illegitimacy and that of her father's position as Supreme Head of the English Church.

While Henry had been getting married Parliament too, under Cromwell's guidance, had been carrying forward what had become the task of creating a secular nation state. It was the turn of the monasteries to receive the government's attention, and the next few years were to witness the chain of events known to history as the Dissolution. The ministrations of Cromwell's agents were the occasion which sparked off into open rebellion the longstanding resentment particularly widespread in the North against, among other things, the religious policies of the King. The revolt, which was called the Pilgrimage of Grace and which lasted throughout the winter of 1536, was finally stamped out by the royal army, led by the Duke of Norfolk (who had been brought out of an enforced retirement especially for this task) early in 1537. The executions and exactions which accompanied the King's resulting displeasure lasted throughout the spring of that year.

These events provided the background to the one occasion on which the Queen attempted to influence the King in political affairs. She is reputed to have begged Henry on her knees to restore the monasteries, whose dissolution had caused the troubles. For her efforts she was told firmly not to meddle in the King's affairs, and to reflect upon the fate of her predecessor as an object lesson in what happened to unruly Queens. The tiff passed over quickly, for by that spring Jane was pregnant. Immediately she was subject to careful attention in order that she should have no reason to lose the child, while on Trinity Sunday a Te Deum was sung to celebrate the Queen's conception. She was confined in the enlarged Palace of Hampton Court, and finally gave birth to a baby boy on 12th October. Henry had been staying at Esher for fear of the plague, and rushed to the Queen's bedside, jubilant at the news. Because of the plague, the infant's christening ceremony was somewhat subdued, but the King's two daughters were nevertheless present to carry their baby brother's train. He was named Edward and to celebrate their kinswoman's success, the Seymour clan were once more advanced in rank and position, Edward Seymour being created Earl of Hertford. The general celebrations which greeted the birth were rather overshadowed, however, by the Queen's death on 24th October. She was buried in St George's Chapel at Windsor; Henry was too overcome with grief even to be present at her funeral.

Left
Henry VII and Elizabeth of York, Henry VIII and Jane Seymour
Just as portraits had been painted of Henry VII and his heirs, together with their mother, so Henry VIII commissioned pictures which showed the continuation of the line. The advantage that he had over his father was that he could now point proudly backwards as well as to the future. It hardly needs pointing out that had Edward died within the lifetime of the King, Jane Seymour would not have figured in these state portraits. Even her appearance in this picture was on trust, since it was painted to presage the birth of a royal heir, a thing which history had shown was no certainty.

Above right
Thomas Cromwell, Earl of Essex (1485?-1540) (after Holbein)
One of the two architects of the Henrician Revolution, Thomas Cromwell, like Cardinal Wolsey before him, rose from humble origin to a position of great power and influence and finally suffered a similar fate; having created the supremacy of the King-in-Parliament, his gracious master, who was his sole support, cast him to the wolves. For Henry sacrificed both Wolsey and Cromwell to shield himself from the opposition that his will aroused. Although he is said to have done it with regret, Henry submitted Cromwell to the final indignity of a public death at Tyburn at the hands of the Norfolk faction.

Below right
The Royal Arms with those of Jane Seymour at Hampton Court
During Henry's reign, Hampton Court was frequently redecorated with new coats of arms and devices. In 1525, when he graciously received this magnificent gift from Cardinal Wolsey, his first act was to order the removal of the Cardinal's emblems and have them replaced by his own. At the same time his initials, together first with those of Queen Catherine, and then those of Anne Boleyn, were carved in many places around the palace to denote the royal occupation. In her turn, Jane Seymour was to see her mark placed on the palace, including the carved beasts placed at the main gate. Because of her unique contribution to the reign, her emblems were to remain.

Above
The Visitation of the Monasteries
The monastic ideal, essentially a medieval phenomenon, was by the 16th century in full decay. Indeed, before the Reformation several of the smaller houses in England had already been dissolved, while the Pope had himself considered and given his assent to a project for doing away with many more, and bringing the religious orders into the regular clergy, so what Cromwell did was not without precedent. Most of the monks thus turned out upon the world were found benefices in the regular Church, while many also received pensions. Some inevitably fell victim to the exigencies of the royal supremacy, and this illustration shows one of Cromwell's men leaving a monastery (probably Colchester) after sacking it, and hanging the abbot.

Below, left and right
The Orders of monks
This illustration from a religious manuscript shows members of the different religious orders active in 16th-century England. Foreign observers often remarked upon the devoutness of the English, citing the frequency with which the people attended mass. Nevertheless it was also true that the clergy had never stood in lower esteem, and by 1529 it is probable that only Wolsey and the conservatism of Henry stood between the clergy and drastic reform. This was not altogether surprising, for despite the feelings which led in part to the Pilgrimage of Grace, the regular clergy and the religious orders represented an enormous financial burden on the lay population, and thus prevented the proper administration of justice.

Above right
Fountains Abbey
The Dissolution was pressed forward, and many people were to profit by it. In most parts of the country the 'bare ruined choirs' themselves disappeared within a few years, as the people used their materials to erect buildings of a more practical value to a secular society.
From an Elizabethan ballad about Walsingham Abbey we learn that:

> 'Level, level with the ground
> The towers do lie,
> Which with their golden glittering tops
> Pierced once to the sky.'

Fountains Abbey in Yorkshire however, survived the depredations of the local population and remains as an imposing ruin, not least among which is the magnificent tower, built during the reign of Henry VII.

Left

Thomas Cranmer, Archbishop of Canterbury (1490-1556)

From lowly origins, Cranmer rose quickly to high office. While Henry was desperately casting about for ways of obtaining his divorce from Catherine, Cranmer, as an obscure Doctor of Theology, proposed a solution: that he should solicit the opinion of the universities to promote his case. Cranmer's extreme compliance with the King's will marked him as the ideal successor to Warham, despite the fact that he had a wife. Once consecrated, he set to work on a task that was to transcend the immediate problem of the divorce and create the theology of the English Church as embodied in the Book of Common Prayer. For his part in this he died a martyr's death in the fires of Mary's reign.

Right above

Stephen Gardiner, Bishop of Winchester (1483?-1555)

While Cranmer was a conforming and compassionate man (he alone interceded with the King on behalf of Anne Boleyn and Cromwell for example) his opponent in the religious struggle unleashed by the Reformation was not. As long as Henry and Edward sat on the throne, Gardiner's unbending conservatism was kept in check, but with the accession of Mary, he came into his own. Henry was well aware of the sort of man he was, and when questioned as to whether he had meant to exclude Gardiner from the Council of Regency, replied: 'I remembered him well enough and of good purpose have left him out'.

Right below

Edward Seymour, Earl of Hertford (1506-52)

Because his sister had died in childbirth, producing the King's only legitimate son Edward remained in favour, and occupied a leading position in the Council after the fall of the Howards. His career reached its peak after Henry's death, when he became Lord Protector of young Edward, and was made Duke of Somerset and Earl Marshal. This success was not to last, however, for he was sent to the Tower in 1549, and although he was released and regained much of his former power, his second fall in 1552 led to his execution by the faction of the Duke of Northumberland, which was later to put Lady Jane Grey on the throne.

Opposite

Thomas Howard, 3rd Duke of Norfolk (1473-1554)

Thomas Howard, who, with Gardiner led the conservative faction against the Reformation, was another difficult character. Unlike Gardiner he was an uneducated man and a soldier rather than a politician. Indeed his conservatism was of an unsophisticated nature; his hatred of the new men who were occupying the posts rightfully, in his view, reserved for the nobility, explains his dismissal of Wolsey as the 'butcher's cur', while his son, the poet Surrey, echoing his father, called Cromwell 'that foul churl'. Indeed, Norfolk was spared the block only by Henry's death, because he had connived at his son's quartering his arms with those of the King.

Anne of Cleves

Great attention was paid to the baby boy and stringent precautions were taken to safeguard his health. Nobody was allowed to go near him without the express permission of the King, and his life was supervised down to the smallest detail. Such precautions indicated that although the royal birth had delighted Henry, it had by no means allayed his fears for the succession. It came as no surprise, therefore, that Henry was before long actively casting about for another wife.

In any case political and diplomatic pressures were forcing him in this direction. Until 1533 Henry had been able to count on Francis I's help against the threat from Charles; in that year however, events in England convinced Francis that he could no longer remain in such an alliance. Accordingly, attempts were made by Cromwell to secure an alliance in Germany but the continuing hostility between France and Spain made these efforts largely unnecessary. The Peace of Nice in the summer of 1538 and the Treaty of Toledo of January 1539 brought about a new situation. This and the efforts of Reginald Pole to raise a crusade against England convinced Cromwell of the need for a German alliance. Despite his master's continuing doubts and the arrival of a French embassy in June, he pressed forward. His plans for a Lutheran alliance against the Pope came to nought, but by October he had persuaded Henry into a marriage alliance with the Duke of Cleves who, though no Lutheran, was at least a prince of what later were to be called Erastian principles. Henry was to marry Anne, the Duke's sister. This need for an anti-Papal alliance was also dictated by domestic events. The forces released by Henry's policy towards the Pope had split the country on religious issues into two hostile camps, the radicals led by Cromwell and Cranmer, and the conservatives led by Stephen Gardiner, Bishop of Winchester, and the Duke of Norfolk. This split had dominated the Parliamentary session of early 1539, and it was a conservative success, notably in the passing of the Six Articles embodying the full Catholic doctrine, which spurred Cromwell on to push Henry into the marriage with Anne of Cleves.

Left
Henry VIII (after Holbein)

Right
Anne of Cleves (1517-57) (Holbein)
Henry's commissioners' report, passed on to him without comment by Cromwell, that the Princess of Cleves outshone the Duchess of Milan 'as golden sun does the silvery moon', was undoubtedly a gross exaggeration. On the other hand Holbein's portrait, and there is no real evidence to suggest that it was not a reasonable likeness, shows that the remarks passed on her looks by those around the King once she had arrived in England were also largely unmerited. Significantly, the only recorded occasion which marred the contentment of her retirement was when she expressed her indignation that Henry should have married Katherine Parr, whom she esteemed much less attractive than herself.

Despite Henry's particularity as to the looks of his wife, the marriage with Anne of Cleves was above all a diplomatic alliance. Even by late 1539 however, events had largely removed the need for this alliance. It is therefore more than possible that Henry's much publicized inability to consummate the union was largely due to his reluctance to commit himself irrevocably to a useless alliance.

This new marriage was by no means the result of a passionate love affair such as Henry had known with Anne Boleyn. Indeed, he had considered at least eight other candidates before lighting upon Anne, and her merits were discussed critically. In the two years since Jane Seymour's death, Henry had made unsuccessful proposals to various princesses of the Hapsburg and Valois lines, there having been no suitable candidate within his realm. Holbein, by now well-established at court, was sent on expeditions to paint many of these princesses, while ambassadors were requested to submit detailed written reports on the ladies in question. At one stage Henry even suggested a 'beauty parade' of the five French princesses from among whom he was currently considering making his choice. The scandalized French turned down this idea. His wooing of Anne was no exception, and Holbein was sent to paint both the Cleves sisters to aid Henry in his choice. Of the two Henry chose Anne, and in spite of the many rumours and reports to the contrary, he seems to have accepted Cromwell's opinion that she was both talented and beautiful.

The lady finally arrived in England at the end of December 1539. So eager was Henry to see his bride for himself that on 1st January he travelled incognito to Rochester Abbey, where Anne was resting before continuing to London for her official reception on 3rd January. His expectations were sadly deceived; instead of the great beauty he found a woman of about thirty, tall and thin, plain of face, and severe of expression. The interview was a failure, for Anne lacked any social grace and in any case could speak no English. Henry returned to London gloomily aware that it was too late to back out of the marriage. After two days of delay, while Henry tried to find a decent way out of the engagement, the marriage was celebrated at Greenwich on 6th January. As Henry told Cromwell on the previous day, 'It was a great yoke to enter into', and the opinion that the marriage could not last spread quickly. This opinion was confirmed when Henry told his gentlemen of the bedchamber that he had not been able to consummate the marriage.

While he saw little of her in bed, so the King saw little of her during the day. Although she developed an interest in music, Anne shared none of the King's pleasures, preferring instead to supervise the care of the royal gardens. Nor, with her limited English, did she take any pleasure in the company of the King's court, and she kept largely to her own household. In any case, by Easter of 1540, the King had been presented with a new mistress.

Predictably, the King's conscience was already troubled by a marriage that was not going to produce any heirs and which had already outlived its political justification, with the break-up of the Franco-Imperial accord. His objection was that Anne had previously been betrothed to the son of the Duke of Lorraine. The solution of the matter should have been easy for Cromwell who had already managed to get rid of two Queens, for now there was no Pope to deal with. In addition the marriage had never been consummated and the Queen was not opposed to an honourable divorce. Yet there was a problem: it appeared likely that Henry would marry his mistress. This was one of the Queen's maids of honour, Katharine Howard, the niece of the Duke of Norfolk, leader of the conservatives and bitter opponent of the King's minister. Although Cromwell had recovered most of his position after the religious division of the country during the previous year (indeed he had been created Earl of Essex and Great Chamberlain on 17th April) he realized that to procure the divorce would lead to a marriage which would inevitably bring about his own downfall at the hands of the Howard faction.

To avoid this Cromwell attempted to purge the conservatives and during May, several of the reactionary bishops and lesser clergy were arrested and put in prison. But while Cromwell had been busy at Westminster, the Howards, left at Greenwich, succeeded in convincing Henry of his minister's heresy. By June they felt strong enough to act, and Cromwell was arrested and put in the Tower. He was condemned unheard of treason and heresy, but kept alive long enough to give testimony enabling the King to gain his divorce. On 23rd July he was executed.

Armed with Cromwell's testimony, Parliament established that the marriage of the King to Anne of Cleves was invalid. With Anne's full agreement, Convocation pronounced the marriage annulled on 9th July. Now no longer his wife Henry adopted Anne as his 'sister' and gave her precedence over all other ladies except the new Queen and his daughters. In addition he settled £500 a year upon her for life and gave her as residences Richmond, Bletchingley Manor and Hever Castle, which had come into his possession on the death of Thomas Boleyn in 1538. Anne was also to keep all her jewels and plate.

The Queen's attitude enabled Henry to carry through this divorce without significant reaction from abroad. Even the Duke of Cleves, though he never gave his official recognition, resigned himself to the inevitable. Anne died in 1557, after seventeen years of comfortable retirement which allowed her to indulge her hitherto frustrated passion for wearing new dresses every day.

Left
Christina of Denmark, Duchess of Milan (Holbein)
Henry was particularly struck by Holbein's portrait of the sixteen year-old widow of Francesco Sforza, Duke of Milan. Christina, however, was less than enthusiastic; although the story that she had said she would only marry Henry if she had had two heads and could thus afford to lose one, is without foundation, it was true that she held Henry personally responsible for the deaths of three wives. In any case the political implications of such a marriage were unwelcome to Christina's uncle, the Emperor Charles V, who had no desire to see Henry involved in the politically sensitive area of the Milanese.

Above left
Self-Portrait by Holbein (1497-1543)
After a first visit in 1526-27 when he painted More and Warham, Holbein returned permanently to England in 1532. By then More was out of favour and Warham dead, but Holbein gained the patronage of Cromwell and through his influence became a paid servant of the King until his death. Although he missed being appointed the King's serjeant-painter only because of his death, Holbein was to produce during this ten-year period a major contribution to the art of the period in painting and design. More important to the historian, he also left an extensive record of the people at the centre of events at a crucial moment of English history.

Above right
Fashion Sketch (Holbein)
Holbein had an eye for detail, as the sheer volume of his sketch-work indicates. Much of this material stemmed from preliminary work for full-scale paintings, and this colour-wash of a man at court around 1540 is one of a whole series of fashion sketches made at this time. It is worth noting the plainness of the clothes worn by this courtier in comparison with the sumptuous apparel of the king in Holbein's portraits. The contrast is hardly surprising, for in the latter case Holbein was making a political statement as much as creating a work of art.

Above left

Henry VIII and his jester, Will Somers
This illustration of Will Somers, the King's fool, listening to his master playing the harp, comes from the King's psalter, made in about 1540. It is probable that Somers entered the King's service around 1525, coming from the household of a merchant from Calais. Over the years Somers established a close rapport with Henry and by the end of the reign he had become his constant companion, alone knowing how to take his mind off the pain caused by his ulcerous leg. Despite his closeness to Henry, it appears that he kept himself apart from political faction, which may well explain his long career in Henry's service.

Above right

Nonesuch Palace
The youthful rivalry with Francis I if anything intensified with the passing years. Predictably, therefore, the construction of the French King's château at Chambord spurred Henry to compete. The result was Nonesuch Palace in Surrey, depicted on this chest, which was begun in 1538. Using the wealth and materials from the monasteries (much religious sculpture has been excavated from the foundation rubble) Henry set out to dazzle Europe, and to do so he called in craftsmen from all over Europe, including the famous Nicolo Bellin of Modena. In fact this royal fun-palace was never completed and has long since disappeared, although recent excavations have started to reveal some of its splendour.

Below left

Cardinal Reginal Pole (d. 1558)
Although descended through the Duke of Clarence from Edward III, Reginald Pole was nevertheless favoured by the King and employed in his service until at least 1536, engaged on missions abroad to secure support for the King's divorce. By 1537 however, Henry was aware that the Cardinal was intriguing against him. In the next year Cardinal Pole began his abortive mission around the courts of Europe to organize a concerted effort to overthrow the King. It was because of this that the Pole family were imprisoned (and Lord Montague executed) in 1538.

Below right

Hever Castle, Kent
Hever Castle, a typical late 15th-century moated country house, entered the possession of the Bullen (Boleyn) family in 1462. At the time of Henry's courtship of Anne, Hever Castle was her home and the scene of many significant events of the period. In 1540, the King placed it at the disposal of his 'sister', Anne of Cleves. Upon her death the castle passed into obscurity, and eventually, decay. Recently the property has been extensively restored and extended.

Katharine Howard

The fact that the King was occupied with a new mistress within a very short time after the Cleves marriage represented the successful culmination of the Duke of Norfolk's continued attempts to reinstate his family fortunes in the royal favour after the set-back occasioned by the fall of his niece, Anne Boleyn. As soon as the marriage alliance with Cleves was confirmed, Norfolk managed to secure two coveted positions as maids-of-honour in the new Queen's household for his nieces Katharine Howard and Mary Norris. In the event the King was struck by the vivacious, well-rounded good looks of Katharine. Norfolk's plans had succeeded to a far greater degree than that for which he had originally hoped, for the King was so enamoured of this young girl (she was about twenty at the time), a passion probably enhanced by the shock his system had received from Anne of Cleves, that he was soon thinking in terms of marriage. Even in September 1540, a month or so after the marriage took place, de Marillac, the French ambassador, was able to report that, 'The King is so amorous of Katharine Howard that he cannot treat her well enough, and caresses her more than he did the others.' Henry himself described Katharine on the coins struck to commemorate the new marriage as 'a blushing rose without a thorn'.

Although her marriage with the King was an unexpected honour, her upbringing made it more than likely that Katharine would fulfil such a role. She was the daughter of Edmund Howard, a younger brother of the Duke of Norfolk, who had neither money nor position. Indeed, he appeared to have been looked on with disfavour by the King and lived his life away from court. Her mother was Joyce Leigh, a rich widow with lands in Kent, who died when Katharine was very small. With the father abroad and mother dead, Katharine and her brothers and sisters were moved to Horsham to be put in the care of the Dowager Duchess of Norfolk, widow of the second Duke. Such a practice was normal with the Howards as all children were regarded as family assets, and brought up accordingly. During her adolescence she was moved to Lambeth House, where she was prepared for a life at court, under the surveillance of the Duke, who throughout this period had managed to cling onto the Lord Treasurer's staff.

After the confusion surrounding the divorce from Anne of Cleves and the death of Cromwell, the Howards came into their own both at court and at Westminster. This rise in the family fortunes was underlined by the fact that Henry married his new bride on 28th July, the very day that Cromwell was beheaded at

Left

Henry VIII (attr. Holbein)
Although only fifty in 1541, Henry was by the standards of the time an old man. The life he had led had dispersed the old charm and youthful vigour, and he was by now severely handicapped in his movements. Nevertheless for a short while his romance with the young Katharine breathed new life into his ageing body. As in his early days, he began a round of feasting and dancing, while he spent the day in the saddle, hunting from dawn to dusk. The discovery that his adored spouse was not the innocent fawn he had supposed came as a bitter shock. While he had rejoiced at Anne Boleyn's fall, now he wept and withdrew from court life.

Right

Katharine Howard (1521?-42)
Although there is no indisputably authenticated contemporary portrait of her, Katharine Howard is generally accepted as having been the most striking of Henry's wives. Certainly those at court thought so, and the Privy Council put their finger on the reasons for the marriage when, during the course of their instructions to Sir William Paget, ambassador to France, they made a remark that: 'The King . . . being solicited by his Council to marry again, took to wife Katharine . . . thinking now in his old age to have obtained a jewel for womanhood, but this joy is turned to extreme sorrow; . . . having heard that she was not a woman of such purity as was esteemed.'

ETATIS   SVA 21

Tyburn. The marriage was celebrated quietly at Oatlands, a manor near Weybridge that Henry had purchased in 1537, and it was a matter of two weeks before public prayers were offered for Queen Katharine at the Chapel Royal. There was however, no mention of a date being set for the Queen's Coronation, although it was generally assumed that this would be announced following news of an eventual pregnancy. Despite a long period of honeymoon spent on a hunting progress, there was no sign of the Queen being with child on their return to court. Henry nevertheless doted upon Katharine, showering her with wealth and costly gifts, and dancing attendance upon her. In December he left for a private visit with the Queen to Oatlands before the start of the Christmas festivities at court.

With the winter drawing to an end there was still no hint of the hoped-for heir. Undeterred the King was planning for the Queen to accompany him on a tour of the defences on the south coast, when he fell ill at the end of February. The ulcers on his leg were exacerbated by this illness and Henry took to his bed, which had an immediate effect upon the court and the Queen. Used to the activity of the honeymoon and to the festivities of the Christmas period, Katharine turned to the young men of the court for amusement while the King was confined to his chamber. It was not until the end of June that the court set off on the royal progress through the north and the midland counties.

This progress of 1541 was in effect the King's reply to the Pilgrimage of Grace; it was the first time a monarch had toured the north for fifty years, and Henry was determined to impress. Consequently the whole episode was one of unparalleled luxury and splendour, and not least among the attractions was the figure of the Queen. Such was the importance given to her place in the events that when the royal party arrived at York in September, it was assumed that the Abbey had been prepared for the long-awaited coronation. (In fact these preparations had been for a meeting with James V of Scotland, who did not arrive.) In any case the Queen had not fulfilled what was the necessary requirement for her coronation, and the progress returned to London with no news of an heir.

Henry could think only of the success of his tour of the north and it was in this mood of elation that he received from Cranmer evidence of gross and perhaps treasonable misconduct on the part of the Queen. The information concerned the period of Katharine's life spent at Horsham and Lambeth House. She was accused of intimacy and acts of impropriety with more than one person but in particular with a young man called Francis Dereham. Dereham claimed that he had been betrothed to Katharine and therefore was not guilty of adultery.

In an effort to clear himself Dereham then accused a man called Thomas Culpepper of having succeeded in the Queen's affections. The investigation into this allegation brought to light evidence of a much more serious nature. It became obvious that an affair had been going on throughout 1541 between this man and the Queen, and that it had even continued during the progress in the north. Lady Rochford was cited as having arranged, or at least having facilitated the meetings between the two. By the time the investigations were completed it was clear that the whole of the Queen's household was involved in some way or other in serious indiscretions. Even the King's niece, Lady Margaret Douglas, was not above reproach.

Unable to accept completely the implications of the evidence laid before him, Henry sent Katharine to Syon House while he made up his mind on what course to take. In December Culpepper and Dereham were hanged, while Parliament finally began to move against the Queen; a Bill of Attainder against her and Lady Rochford was passed in January. Katharine was brought to the Tower and with Lady Rochford, now insane with fear, she was beheaded on 12th February.

Despite Katharine's plea for their safety, Henry had several of the Howards, including the ageing Dowager Duchess, arrested on charges of misprision of treason. They were soon released, but it was the end of the Norfolks' influence at court, although the Duke, by turning on his niece, had managed to retain his state of office. On the eve of the King's death six years later, the family received another blow to its fortunes when the Duke's son Henry, the Earl of Surrey, was attainted for treason and executed early in 1547. Norfolk himself escaped a similar fate only because the King died before the order could be issued, but he spent the whole of Edward VI's reign in the Tower, never to return to public life.

Above left

Henry presenting a Charter to the Company of Barber Surgeons (Holbein)
When in 1541, the King granted a charter to the liveried company of Barber Surgeons, the company commissioned Hans Holbein to commemorate the event with a painting. Although the work was to be one of Holbein's last (the artist died before a second version of the painting was complete), it expressed a theme that ran through all the Holbein paintings of the King. Surrounded by his dutiful subjects, Henry sits aloof in regal majesty upon a throne holding the sword of state. Holbein's work represented the claims of Henry VIII's monarchy.

Below left

One of Henry's Galleys
The preparations for war during these years were not confined to shore defences; Henry had always been interested in naval matters, indeed he had grown up at Greenwich within sight of the naval dockyards, and this interest was reflected in the attention he gave to re-equipping the fleet, including this ship. As the emphasis in naval warfare shifted away from fire-power to speed, ships were rebuilt as one hundred tonners, with only 122 guns. The picture is taken from a naval roll of 1546.

Above right

Deal Castle, Kent

Below right

St Mawes Castle, Cornwall
Throughout the 1530's Henry had been remarkably free from foreign pressure; he had pursued his politics at home secure in the knowledge that with France and Spain at loggerheads there was no threat of interference from outside. The Treaty of Toledo, concluded in January 1539, created a dangerous situation however. This, together with the fact that Pope Paul III had put the Papal Bull of Excommunication into execution, and with the activities of Reginald Pole, convinced Henry that the time had come to create a strong defence system along the south coast. Much of the wealth coming out of the monasteries went to financing this operation which lasted for about three years. Although the local population was turned out to build earthworks on the east coast, the major works stretched from the Thames Estuary to the Cornish coast. This consisted of a network of coastal forts linked by land and sea routes. In some instances, existing castles were extended and modified to take modern armaments, but many new castles were built, including those at Deal and St Mawes. Much of the work was supervised by a German engineer, Stephan van Haschenperg. The type of fort he created had not been seen before in Britain and was organized specifically for cannon warfare.

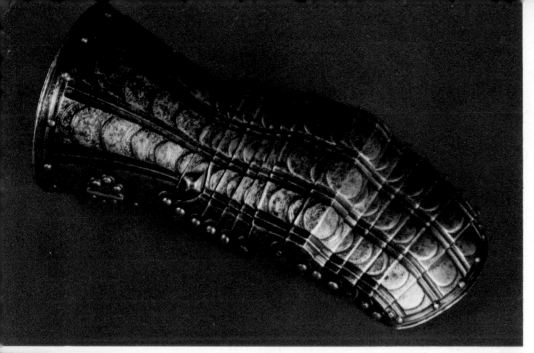

Above left
Henry VIII's Gauntlet
This Greenwich mitten-gauntlet is embossed with scale patterns and etched with fluted bands. The knuckles are decorated with the Tudor Rose. Although it is not certain that it was made for Henry VIII, the opinion of a French writer early this century that it was 'fait pour un grand patronage, de corpulence très au-dessus de la moyenne . . .' substantiates the claim.

Right
Margaret Pole, Countess of Salisbury (1473-1541)
Reginald Pole's indiscretions around the courts of Europe had already sent his brother, Lord Montague, to the block, and had condemned his mother to two years' confinement in the Tower. Here she was well treated, but she nevertheless remained in danger from a suspicious King who had already lived up to his early claim that there was in the country 'no head so noble but that he would make it fly'. The Countess was no exception, for before Henry set out on his progress of the North, he determined to clear the Tower to secure the capital at his back. Accordingly the old lady was brought from the Tower on 27th May to be executed on Tower Green.

Centre left
The Haunted Gallery, Hampton Court
The history of Henry's marriage to Katharine Howard has provided England with one of its most famous ghost stories. When Cramner broke the news of his wife's infidelities to the King, the court was in residence at Hampton Court. Katharine was placed under guard at the palace while Henry awaited the results of the commission of enquiry into the allegations against her. Overcome by the possibility of Katharine's faithlessness, Henry shut himself away and refused to see the Queen. When she tried to reach his chambers to plead her innocence she was seized and dragged away screaming along this gallery. The legend that her ghost repeats this event survives.

Below left
The Traitor's Gate, The Tower of London
This gate was known originally as the Water Gate since it gave onto the river and was the entrance for the frequent traffic which came by boat from Greenwich and Westminster. By the middle years of the century it had gained its sinister nickname because of the sombre events which accompanied the Henrician Revolution. Anne Boleyn and Katharine Howard were two among the throng of famous people who entered the Tower for the last time by this Gate.

Katherine Parr

Henry took the news of Katharine's adultery hard, and for nearly eighteen months he remained single; when he did marry again he took a wife more fitting to his position as an ageing widower. Katherine Parr was in all respects a different person to Katharine Howard. Although much younger than Henry she was nevertheless over thirty at the time of their marriage in June 1543, and had already been widowed twice. Her first marriage had ended in 1529 when she was seventeen and had produced no children. Between the years 1540 and 1541 she served in the household of Katharine Howard as Lady Latymer, her second husband not dying until March 1543. It was while she was thus at court that Katherine became known to the King, although there was no hint of any interest on his part. With the fall of the Queen, she returned to Yorkshire to supervise the upbringing of her step-children. On the death of her husband she was back at court, and was shortly involved with Sir Thomas Seymour, the younger brother of the Earl of Hertford and an uncle of the Duke of Cornwall. She must have made some impression upon the King, however, for within three months of Latymer's death she turned away Seymour who discreetly returned abroad on a diplomatic mission for the King, and married Henry.

That she meant more to Henry than a prospective mother of further royal children (although she was still well within child-bearing age) may be seen in the fact that she gave him no such heirs and yet managed to survive the King without having lost his affection. It is obvious that Henry saw in her a companion for his old age and a stepmother for his children. By her up-bringing she was suited admirably to such a role, for Katherine was a highly educated and cultured woman while she had already proved her worth in the care of step-children. In spite of her second husband's involvement in the Pilgrimage of Grace she herself tended in religious matters to favour a middle course similar to that of Cranmer. From her religious writings it is obvious that she agreed neither with the conservatives nor with the Lutherans: in her best known work *The Lamentations of a Sinner*, she lauds the manner in which Henry had managed to steer the English Church between two extremes. At Snape Hall she provided a centre for many scholars of a reforming turn of mind, and this continued when she had her household at court. This reputation for liberal learning and moderate reform in religious matters spread abroad and incited the conservatives — led now by Gardiner and Wriothesley — to intrigue against her. In 1546 the trial and burning of Anne Askew for heresy provided the occasion for action, particularly as, according to John Foxe, the King and Katherine were on bad terms, due to her outspokenness in such matters. It appears that the outraged Henry had actually been contradicted by his wife. Armed with evidence of her suspected heresy and authority apparently signed by Henry himself, Wriothesley came to arrest the Queen, only to find that a reconciliation had been effected. He was roundly abused for his pains by an irritable monarch. In matters of lay education it was probably Katherine's influence that was

Left
Henry VIII in old age
Henry's increasing ill-temper in his later years was largely the product of his physical disability, and particularly the ulcer on his leg, which at times rendered him speechless with pain. This ulcer and his great weight prevented him from walking freely, and around 1545 he began to be carried everywhere in a sedan chair. This must have taken some lifting, for contemporary accounts have left a wealth of comment on his size. According to Fuller, 'he had a body and a half, very abdominous and unwieldy with fat. And it was death for him to be dieted, so great was his appetite, and death to him not to be dieted, so great his corpulency.'

Right
Katherine Parr (1512-48)
When Henry married again in July, 1543, it was to the general surprise of the court. It was obvious however, that this sixth marriage was for Henry a bid for companionship in his old age. And the fact that Katherine bore him no children during those final years of his life did not disturb their union, for she was well able to manage the irascible old man. Indeed, Henry expressed himself well-pleased with this last wife and in his will gave testimony to 'the great love, obedience, chastity of life and wisdom being in our wife and Queen'.

KATHARINE PARRE

behind the revival of royal interest in the seats of higher learning. The universities were spared the worst exactions of the King's commissioners, and Henry endowed several new colleges, particularly those of Christchurch at Oxford and Trinity at Cambridge.

It was with Katherine's accession as Queen that the children of Henry came closest to experiencing a real family life. Elizabeth and Edward had not known their mothers, while Mary, who was twenty before her mother died, had spent many years in enforced separation from both her parents. Katherine Parr however, brought the two younger children into her own household and supervised their education. Although those who were responsible for the royal children's education were by no means men whom Henry would have regarded as heretics, nor yet were they conservatives, and the influence they had on Elizabeth and Edward was reflected in the events of the years which succeeded that of Henry's death. Mary however, was only four years younger than Katherine, and by 1543 her moral and intellectual development were already complete. Yet though she maintained a separate household she remained on the friendliest terms with the Queen, who took a close interest in her physical and material well-being.

Henry and Katherine were married at Hampton Court by Stephen Gardiner on 12th June 1543. Shortly afterwards they set off via Oatlands on a royal progress through southern England. This travelling characterized much of the life that Katherine led as Queen, for Henry managed, until the final months of his life, to overcome the constant ill-health from which he suffered during this period in order to be on the move fulfilling his royal duties around the country. Katherine accompanied him, acting not only as Queen, but also as nurse; a role which she also performed at court, as in the spring of 1544, when in the middle of preparations for war against the French, Henry was confined to bed by his ulcerated legs. On this occasion Katherine moved her bed to an antechamber off the King's bedroom in order to nurse him properly. When Henry had recovered he insisted on going to France himself to take part in the campaign of 1544, and Katherine was left as Regent for three months.

On his return from France, Henry's health began to deteriorate. Though it did not prevent him from performing his duties, it was becoming increasingly apparent that Katherine's career as Queen would be cut short by her husband's death. The royal progress of 1545 was successfully accomplished but that of the following year had to be cut short in July. In the autumn Henry was well enough to go hunting, but by November he was back at Whitehall receiving treatment for his health and particularly for his legs. For some time the state of his legs had made it necessary for him to be carried about at court in a sort of sedan-chair.

By the end of 1546 the King's health made it necessary to bring his will up to date. The succession had already been settled by Act of Parliament in 1544, naming Edward, Mary and Elizabeth in that order as his heirs. The fact that Edward was only nine years old in 1546 made it necessary to provide for a Council of Regency. This was done on 26th December. Henry was well aware of the hostilities that divided his court, and had consequently left out the names of extremists, such as Gardiner, from the list of Councillors. One other surprising omission was the name of the Queen, Katherine, although the will paid tribute to a wise and virtuous life and left her with a considerable sum in plate, jewelry and money.

This, and the fact that Katherine, together with the royal children, had been kept from the King during the final months of his life, effectively brought her public life to an end; when Henry died on 28th January it was Cranmer and the politicians who were with him. The following month, Henry was buried at St George's Chapel, Windsor, and laid to rest in Jane Seymour's grave as he had commanded.

His death was to herald a period of great anxiety for those in public life. Yet despite the factional quarrels and bloodshed which rent the court and the country during the succeeding years, the provisions of Henry's Act of Succession were to be upheld (apart from the nine-day reign of Lady Jane Grey) only to be superseded by the accession of the House of Stuart in the next century.

As for Katherine Parr, she retired into private life, marrying early in the same year of the King's death the dubious Thomas Seymour, who four years earlier, had withdrawn his suit for this rich widow to make way for the King; but within eighteen months of her fourth and final marriage, she died on 5th September 1548.

Left
Henry VIII's last armour
This suit of armour was made about the time of Henry's last venture abroad during the war with France in 1544. Its very size illustrates how large the King had become even then. On his return the enforced inactivity caused by renewed ill-health increased his girth still further.

Above
Sir William Butts (d. 1545)
As Henry's health deteriorated, so he relied increasingly on the ministrations of his medical entourage, which was led by Sir William Butts. Butts was one of the leading figures of the humanist tradition (among his protégés was Sir John Cheke) and his death early in 1545, removed one of the strongest reforming influences from the court. His influence was all the more important since by the early 1540's he was for long periods in permanent attendance upon the King.

Below left
Princess Elizabeth
Elizabeth was not quite ten years old in 1543. Despite her age she had developed a remarkable capacity for scholarship, and particularly for languages, of which she was later to speak several with complete fluency. In fact this talent had emerged even earlier, yet it was not until Katherine Parr took her education in hand that it was shaped by the influence of Sir John Cheke and Roger Ascham. Before the end of the year the Princess was translating foreign works of considerable length. At Christmas, for example, she presented Katherine with a translation of a devotional work by Margaret of Navarre.

Below right
Prince Edward
Catherine Parr was also responsible for bringing Prince Edward (not quite six at the time of her marriage) from the royal manors in the Home Counties, where he had been sent by Henry for fear of the plague. He was given a suite next to the Queen's so that she could oversee his daily routine. She also had Cheke appointed as his tutor. It was fortunate for Edward that he was naturally attracted to books and scholarship, for he was subjected from the age of six to a rigorous routine of hard work, and given a thorough grounding in both classical and modern languages. In addition he was schooled in the Scriptures, in philosophy and in 'the liberal sciences'.

Right
Princess Mary
By the time of Henry's marriage to Katherine Parr, Mary was twenty-seven years of age. Although the reconciliation with her father had brought Mary out of the exile to which her refusal to deny the validity of her mother's marriage had consigned her, she was by no means a happy woman. From a very early age she had been used as a diplomatic counter in the interests of Henry's European ambitions. Even her friendship with Katherine Parr did not take her mind from her own continuing spinsterhood, and as she herself observed, 'While my father lives I shall be only the Lady Mary, the most unhappy lady in Christendom.'

ANNO DNI · 1 5 4 4 ·

LADI MARI   DOVGHTER TO

THE MOST   VERTVOVS PRINCE

KING HENRI   THE EIGHT

THE AGE OF   XXVIII YERES

Left

Sir John Cheke (1514-47)

Sir John Cheke became a trusted servant of the young King, and was rewarded for his services by being made Secretary of State in 1553. But Cheke's contribution was more profound in the field of scholarship: for example, he was the first Professor of Greek at Cambridge. When the university was threatened by the King's commissioners during the dissolution of the monasteries, Cheke was among those men who stood up to the King's designs and thereby saved the university.

Above right

Sir Thomas Seymour (d. 1549)

Sir Thomas Seymour, who became Lord High Admiral after the death of the King, did not long survive his wife. Jealous of his brother's power, he used his position as Admiral to build up funds to finance his penchant for intrigue. With no political skill he soon fell victim to the climate of the times and was executed. The Princess Elizabeth, as ward of the Dowager Queen Katherine Parr, had conducted a some-what scandalous flirtation with Seymour, and provided him with his epitaph. When she was informed of his execution she made the comment: 'This day died a man of much wit and very little judgment'.

Below left

Hatfield Old House

Originally built for the bishops of Ely in 1496, this large house was seized by Henry during the Reformation. It became the principal residence of Henry's children, especially Edward and Elizabeth, and it was at Hatfield that Elizabeth held her first Council. The house became the property of the Cecil family during James I's reign.

Below right

The death of Henry VIII

This picture from the reign of Edward VI was probably painted in 1548 to commemorate Cranmer's order for the destruction of religious images. Through the window (top right) men may be seen carrying out this work. At the foot of the throne on which Edward sits, the idolatrous and superstitious Pope collapses before the true word of God, as pronounced by the supreme Head of His Church in England. For Edward has received his title by rightful succession. His faithful Council look on with righteous approval. Standing is Somerset, and sitting next to him are Northumberland, Cranmer and Bedford.

Left

Katherine Parr's room, Sudeley Castle, Gloucestershire

Shortly after Henry's death, Katherine Parr married for the fourth time. Her new husband was Thomas Seymour, who had stepped aside when the King announced his intention of marrying Katherine. The marriage was held in secret, and when Seymour's brother, The Lord Protector, learned of it, he was much annoyed. However, the couple retired to Sudeley Castle, the Seymours' manor, where Katherine finally became a mother in August of the following year. She did not survive the birth and died on 5th September, 1548; she was buried at the castle.

Acknowledgments

The publishers would like to thank the following for their kind permission to reproduce the illustrations in this book:

Reproduced by Gracious Permission of Her Majesty the Queen: 2-3, 4-5, 10-11, 15 below (from Sir Thomas Wriothesley's Manuscript), 16-17, 24-25, 31, 32-33, 34, 37 (Inv. No. 12263), 42 below (Inv. No. 12250), 46, 51, 62 middle, 66, 68 left, endpapers; The College of Arms: 1, 14 above and below, 30 below left (Photo: Brian Morris); Courtesy of Lord Astor of Hever: 23 below left, 35, 36, 39 below, 40 above right and below, 41, 58, 62 above; The Bodleian Library: 10 left (Photo: Nicholas Servian, Woodmansterne Limited), 28 below (Cavendish 'Life of Wolsey' Roll 214.5); The Trustees of the British Museum: 15 above, 18, 40 above left, 48 above, 55 right, 56 above; Courtesy of the Archbishop of Canterbury, Lambeth Palace: 29, 56 above; Department of the Environment: 61 above and below, 62 below; By Permission of the Syndics of the Fitzwilliam Museum, Cambridge: 22; Giraudon: 53; Sonia Halliday: 23 below right, 38 below (King's College, Cambridge); Michael Holford: 39 above, 60 below, 70 below; Angelo Hornak: 7 below, 23 below left, 30 above, 35, 36, 38 above, 39 below, 40 above right and below, 41, 58, 62 above; A. F. Kersting: 8 both, 42 above, 49 above, 57 below, 72; Kunsthistorisches Museum, Vienna: 13, 45; Kunstmuseum, Basel: 68 right; Magdalen College, Oxford: 9 below; Maison Dieu, Dover: 23 below right; Mas: 9 above, 27; Courtesy of the Trustees of the National Gallery, London: 54; National Portrait Gallery, London: 7 above left, 11 right, 12 left, 21, 23 above right, 30 below right, 43, 47 above, 50 left and below right, 63, 64, 65, 67, 69, 71 both; National Trust, Hardwick Hall: 50 above right (Photo: Jeremy Whitaker); Public Record Office: 26 left; Courtesy of Lord Sandys: 70 above; Scala: 20, 26 right, 52; Spectrum Colour Library: 47 below; St John's College, Cambridge: 7 right, 28 above; Royal College of Surgeons: 60 above; Thyssen-Bornemisza Collection, Lugano: 44; The Toledo Museum of Art, Ohio, Gift of Edward Drummond Libbey: 59; Trinity College, Dublin: 48-49 below; Courtesy of Sir Harry Verney: 7 below left; Victoria & Albert Museum: 6, 12 right, 57 above (Photo: John Webb): Wallace Collection: 55 left (Photo: John Freeman); Courtesy of Earl of Yarborough: 19.

Jacket illustrations:
Front   Henry VIII (Holbein). Thyssen-Bornemisza Collection, Lugano;
Back   Cardinal Wolsey. National Portrait Gallery;
Front Flap   Catherine of Aragon. Kunsthistorisches Museum, Vienna;
Back Flap   Anne Boleyn's Gateway, Hampton Court. Photo: Michael Holford.

Endpapers: Embarkation of Henry VIII.